PYRAMIDS
Tombs for Eternity

PYRAMIDS
Tombs for Eternity

Mildred Mastin Pace

Illustrated by Radu Vero
and Mirela Zisu

McGraw-Hill Book Company

NEW YORK   ST. LOUIS   SAN FRANCISCO   AUCKLAND   BOGOTÁ
GUATEMALA   HAMBURG   JOHANNESBURG   LISBON   LONDON   MADRID
MEXICO   MONTREAL   NEW DELHI   PANAMA   PARIS   SAN JUAN
SÃO PAULO   SINGAPORE   SYDNEY   TOKYO   TORONTO

Library of Congress Cataloging in Publication Data

Pace, Mildred Mastin.
  Pyramids: tombs for eternity.

  Bibliography: p.
  Includes index.
  SUMMARY: Discusses how the pyramids of Egypt were built and what they
looked like in their original state and explores the various theories about pyramids and their "powers."
  1. Pyramids—Egypt—Juvenile literature.   2. Egypt—Antiquities—Juvenile literature.   [1. Pyramids.   2. Egypt—Antiquities]   I. Title.
DT63.5.P3   932   79-11999
ISBN 0-07-048054-0

Book design by Jean Krulis

23456789 BPBP 876543

Contents

Acknowledgments

On my two trips to Egypt to study the pyramids, I was lucky.

First, shortly after arriving in Cairo, I met Kamal el Mallakh, the archeologist who discovered Cheops's boat buried near the Great Pyramid and knows the Giza pyramid complex intimately. Not only his knowledge, but his enthusiasm for the subject he knows so well was a great inspiration. I returned home to start research and to plan this book. Later, when I went back to Egypt to learn more about pyramids, Kamal again took time from his crowded schedule to help. Especially appreciated were the hours we spent in Giza examining Cheops's boat, as he told me the details of its discovery and reconstruction. And always to be remembered is our visit to the workshop-home of Ahmed Youssef Moustafa in the desert near the Great Pyramid, to meet and talk with the genius who had been able to put the boat together again.

Up the Nile, in all the places with their ancient names—Saqqara, Memphis, Dashur, Meidum, Karnak, Thebes—busy people, important people, took time to share their knowledge and lead me into the past. I wish it were possible to thank each one separately.

Mohamed El-Saghir, Director of Antiquities of Upper Egypt, made the ancient wonders of that area available to me, giving his time and that of his staff whenever needed. In Karnak, El Sayd Abd El Hamid, Inspector of Antiquities, was ever helpful, even supplying me with a vehicle geared for desert driving so I could reach out-of-the-way places. And it was at Karnak that Dr. Donald B. Redford of the University of Toronto gave my husband and me the rewarding experience of joining him and his team of young archeologists at their "digs," an excavation of the Akhenaten temple.

Working and researching in Egypt were facilitated, and made more pleasant, by Dr. Thomas Wood and his wife, Deloris, who both taught at the American University in Cairo. They took us into their home and let us make it our base while traveling in Egypt. Since they both had mastered the awesome task of driving in Cairo traffic and knew the city and its environs well, they were most helpful in getting us places we needed to be. In addition, it was the Woods who arranged for my using the University library, where I had access to the archeological collection and books on Ancient Egypt.

I could not have written this book without extensive use of libraries. For, especially when the subject is an ancient one, the richest sources of information are the writings of scholars who have explored the subject and reported their findings. These works are not always easy to come by. Some I needed were written more than a hundred years ago.

Again, I was lucky. In New York City, fifty miles from my home, the New York Public Library has a special division with a vast collection of books on Ancient Egypt. There, in a quiet room, I and other researchers could work without interruption. For that, and for the staff members, always willing and tireless in finding the needed books, I will be ever grateful. Closer to home, the staff of The Butterfield Memorial Library in Cold Spring, N.Y., a member of the Mid-Hudson Library Association, performed miracles in tracking down hard-to-find books for my use.

Once more Kenneth Jay Linsner, who worked with me on "Wrapped for Eternity, The Story of the Egyptian Mummy," was a great help, offering ideas and suggestions and reading the manuscript for accuracy.

Through almost four years of research and writing, my editor at McGraw-Hill, Eleanor Nichols, aided and abetted. To her and her associate, Margaret Regan, my thanks. They were very patient.

Mildred Mastin Pace

Foreword

According to Plutarch, that popular Roman writer and intellectual of the first century A.D., the pyramid was the "first of all forms." Whether we agree or not, it is certain that the pyramid is the first form we think of when anyone mentions Egypt, ancient or modern. The towering structures of stone at Giza come to mind at once, although these monuments to Cheops, Chephren, and Mycerinus, built in the third millennium B.C., are not the earliest or only pyramids. There are many more, as you will learn in this book, and each has its own story.

Ever since their construction, these awesome tombs have acted as magnets, drawing the famous, the infamous, and the anonymous. Generations of curious visitors literally have left marks upon their stones.

11

Need one question why the pyramid has been used to symbolize dominion over the four quarters of the earth? From Alexander the Great to Napoleon, warriors and intellectuals have paid homage at the foot of these structures and, from time to time, have visited the chambers within.

The story of the pyramids is also the story of ordinary people. Accounts of the daily lives of the builders and later of the excavators provide fascinating reading. A certain type of investigator has always been drawn to the pyramids of Egypt: the nineteenth century brought speculators, treasure-seekers, and savants, and the twentieth century has seen the arrival of mystics, UFO hunters, astrologists, and occultists. Often called "pyramidiots," these people have produced more literature about their "discoveries" than scholarly investigators and archeologists have.

But it is no wonder that these monuments have attracted so much attention. Their colossal scale, history, and antiquity are surpassed only by their ability to inspire the romantic. By day these sentinels loom above laughing visitors, but by night their black triangular shapes act to connect heaven to earth, fulfilling their ancient purpose and turning the frivolous sightseer into a contemplative admirer. Under such circumstances the naturally active human mind begins to work overtime.

More than seventy pyramids have been identified from Abu Rouash in the north, to the "Ethiopian" pyr-

12

amids of the northern Sudan in the south. Many more may lie hidden under desert sands, waiting to be discovered by young archeologists.

Pyramids are important to our understanding of Egyptian thought and art. They testify to the Egyptian love of stone for its durable qualities. The Egyptian longing for everlasting life is reflected in these pyramids, which already have stood for millennia and most probably will continue to stand for millennia to come. Building them was a remarkable attempt to overcome death and time by a civilization undaunted by these prospects. Time is not eternity, however. Who can guarantee that Egypt's monuments will not collapse as the result of some unforeseen catastrophe? They have already suffered much from vandalism, plundering, and natural weathering. In "The Teaching for Merikare," an Egyptian papyrus that comes down to us from ca. 2100 B.C., we read: "Do not put your trust in the length of years/The council which judges regards a lifetime as an hour." Surely then a thousand years is but a day.

It is hoped that this book will provide a basis for further study and investigation of the pyramids by eager future archeologists. New chapters can then be written in the tale of these monuments, while they are still here for us to examine.

Kenneth Jay Linsner
Curator, The Kraemer Collection
Department of Classics
New York University
Director, The American Center
for Conservation of Art and Antiquities

The first known stone structures, erected by Imhotep for the Pharaoh Zoser, were the Step Pyramid, a burial place for the Pharaoh, and the surrounding complex of ceremonial buildings. With these structures began the Pyramid Age, whose most important examples were completed in less than 200 years:

PHARAOH	DYNASTY III.	LOCATION	DIMENSION OF BASE
Zoser (Step Pyramid)	(c. 2680 to 2570 B.C.)	Saqqara	411 ft. E.-W. to 358 ft. N.-S.
Sekhem-Khet (Buried Pyramid)	"	Saqqara	395 ft. square
	IV.		
Seneferu (?)	(c. 2570 to 2450 B.C.)	Meidum	473 ft. square
Seneferu (Bent Pyramid)	"	Dahshur	620 ft. square
Seneferu (Northern Pyramid)	"	Dahshur	719 ft. square
Cheops (Great Pyramid)	"	Giza	756 ft. square
Chephren	"	Giza	709 ft. square
Mycerinus	"	Giza	356 ft. square

But even with Mycerinus's pyramid, the careful work of the builders had begun to decline. Although many more pyramids were built in later years, the scale became less grand and the workmanship less and less proficient. While some of these later pyramids contain invaluable archeological relics, they hardly rival the awe-inspiring earlier structures.

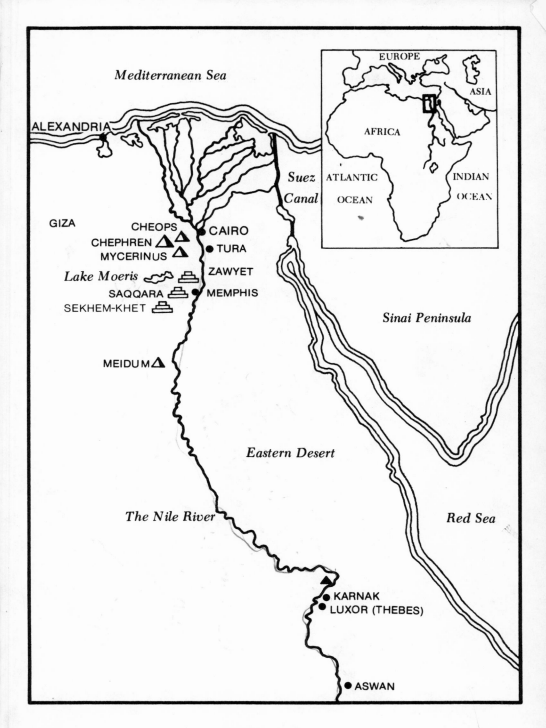

Fig. 1. The Egyptian Pyramids.

PYRAMIDS
Tombs for Eternity

1
Stones for a Pharaoh

The sun was hot, the desert air still, and there was no shade where the young man stood. As far as he could see there was only sand and sky and the fierce, bright light of the sun. The sand burned through the soles of his light sandals and rose in small, hot puffs at his every step. But he decided to walk once more around the piece of land he had chosen. He had to be sure.

It was a rectangular shape and covered eighteen thousand square yards on a large plateau at Saqqara. He stopped to look down when he reached the eastern edge of the site. Below he saw the River Nile and its valley, and the capital city of Memphis. The White City, it was called. And the immense wall encircling it, the king's palace, the temples and mansions with their whitewashed surfaces, shimmered in the sun.

It pleased Imhotep to think that everyone in Memphis who looked his way could see the plateau where he was standing.

This was the proper site for the tomb. It lay on the west bank of the Nile, where royal tombs were always built, since the Land of the Dead was westward, beyond the sunset. And under the deep covering of sand, Imhotep knew, was solid rock. The sand could be hauled away. The rock was important to Imhotep's daring plan.

Imhotep was the king's architect and the plan had been taking shape in his mind since the pharaoh, Zoser, had asked him to prepare a tomb for his burial.

Not that the king expected to die soon! He was a young man, about the same age as his friend Imhotep. But a pharaoh's tomb—his Castle of Eternity—was an important structure. Many years and the talent of many men were needed for building it, decorating it, and outfitting it with all the objects the king would need in the next world. So the pharaoh had consulted Imhotep about his tomb early in his reign, which began around 2680 B.C.

Imhotep was a young man of many talents. He already held the position of royal scribe in a land where the written word was highly esteemed and copious records were kept. He was a noted astronomer in a society where the accurate observation of the heavens

was a serious study. He was also a physician and a ritu-
alist priest in the royal temple. The son of a famous architect, as long as he could remember he had been ab-
sorbed by the study of building design and construction.

It was Imhotep's genius as an architect and designer that Zoser valued most.

When Imhotep looked down at Memphis he was
aware that it was a city built entirely of mud bricks. It
was a white city only because its important structures
were covered with a coating of white plaster. Everything—including the wall, and the houses of both rich
and poor—was made of mud. The mud, taken from the
Nile, was mixed with a little straw, molded into bricks,
and dried in the sun. Some of the finest buildings were
Imhotep's own work, and many had been built by his
father. All were built of mud brick. None of them
would last.

There was stone aplenty in Egypt. The large plateau where Imhotep stood was solid gray limestone beneath the sand. And across the Nile, a short distance
from Memphis, at Tura, were quarries of fine white
limestone. Imhotep knew, too, that far up the Nile, five
hundred miles away near Aswan, pink granite was to
be had. He had seen it there. For like many Egyptians,
whose only highway was the Nile and a boat their only
means of travel, he had sailed all the way there, to the
first cataract and back.

Actually, mud brick was a practical building material in this desert land of heat and sun. Almost no rain fell and few trees grew. And brick had served the Egyptians well.

The homes of the poor were made entirely of mud. In the homes of the rich and noble, some wood was used—for casement windows and doorways, to give airiness and distinction to a room. Wood was too scarce in Egypt to be used for building. Sometimes a piece of stone would be added to give a touch of elegance. But stone was never used as a structural material.

On the plateau at Saqqara, to the north of the site Imhotep had selected, were the tombs, or *mastabas*, of earlier kings and nobles.

These too were built of mud brick.

Aboveground, the mastaba was a rectangular structure, the mud brick whitewashed and sometimes decorated with geometric patterns in colors. Beneath this, underground, was a burial chamber and usually one or more rooms to hold various objects—furniture, wine jars, vessels for food, and other things the deceased would need for life in the next world. This substructure was also built of mud brick, although in rare cases the burial chamber might be lined with stone as ornamentation.

Imhotep wanted to build a special tomb for Zoser, different from the tomb of any pharaoh of the past. He wanted it to be more than a tomb. He wanted it to be a permanent monument to Zoser's greatness and his glorious reign.

Imhotep's design was revolutionary. Instead of the rectangular shape of the mastaba, his was a massive square. Even more daring, it would not be built of mud brick. It would be built of stone!

Native gray limestone could be quarried from the plateau. There were men who knew how to quarry and cut it. Stone had been used in Egypt for statues long before Zoser's time. But an edifice of stone was unheard of.

Even Imhotep did not know when he planned the stone tomb that he had begun the building of Egypt's first pyramid and the first stone structure in the world.

The building of the stone mastaba would require a tremendous labor force. Imhotep's plans and design were ambitious. The mastaba would stand in the center of the site, an enormous square, each side 207 feet long. It would rise to a height of twenty-six feet. Several thousand workers, at least, would be needed to quarry the stone, cut it, transport it, trim and smooth it. And more men would be needed to put it in place.

Zoser's reign had started well and gave great promise. Egypt was united and at peace. Zoser was willing to give Imhotep all the men he needed for the building of his tomb.

Excitement ran high when construction started. Though the people trusted Imhotep's ability, he was trying something that had never been done before, piling stone upon stone. Stone was heavy. And no one, not even Imhotep, knew how much stress and strain it

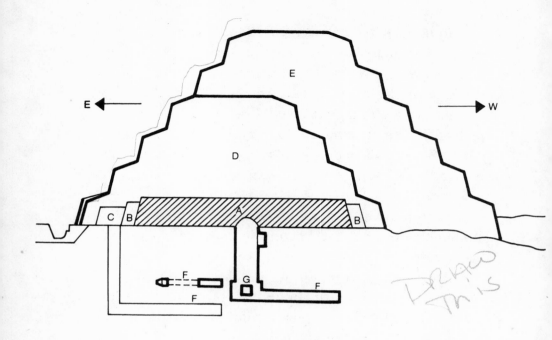

Fig. 2. The development of Zoser's Step Pyramid from the original mastaba. To each side of the mastaba (A), Imhotep added an extension (B) 2 feet lower than the mastaba and 14 feet long, creating a giant step. Then, dissatisfied with the structure's square shape, he extended the east side by 28 feet (C), creating a rectangular structure. Fired by ambition, he added a four-step pyramid (D) and later two more steps (E), raising the pyramid to its full six steps. Meantime, a complicated substructure (F) of shafts, corridors, rooms, and galleries, including Zoser's burial chamber (G), was cut deep in the rock below the pyramid.

could take. Wouldn't the stone on top break the stone beneath it? But as Zoser's mastaba began to rise, doubts were replaced by wonder.

Imhotep had to learn as he went along. He had no precedent for the way stone blocks were raised and placed and fitted together. If one method was not practicable he devised another. And as he learned, he taught others.

Furthermore, he was working with the largest labor force ever known in Egypt. There was no precedent, either, for directing and dealing with large masses of workmen. Their work had to be organized so that production moved steadily without delay from the quarries to the building site.

When the mastaba was finally finished, it was an imposing structure. The great monument covered an area of more than 42,000 square feet and rose, as Imhotep planned, twenty-six feet high. People gazed up at it from the capital city below and the Nile valley. And there was an endless procession climbing the slope up to the plateau to marvel at close range.

The most important part of the whole structure lay hidden far below, at the bottom of a deep shaft cut in the limestone plateau. It was unseen except by those who had built it.

This was the burial chamber. Here, after death, the great Zoser would "live" forever. Imhotep wanted this most sacred place to be beautiful. He remembered the pink granite he had seen in the quarries at Aswan.

That was the stone he wanted for the burial chamber and for a small room to be built directly above it.

Blocks of the pink stone were brought down by boat, five hundred miles from Aswan to Memphis. There they were transferred onto sledges and dragged up the steep slope to the top of the plateau.

When the burial chamber was finished, a round hole cut into the stone ceiling opened into the small room above. Imhotep had a granite plug carved precisely to fit the hole. The plug was six feet long and weighed three tons. It would be stored in the upper room until the day of Zoser's burial. Then it would be put in place, sealing the chamber where the pharaoh lay so he would be safe forever.

There also had to be space, deep down in the tomb, for all the objects Zoser would need for his personal use in the next world. So Imhotep had four long galleries hewn out of the stone near the burial chamber; these were handsomely decorated with blue tiles, panels, and reliefs carved on the stone walls. These rooms would hold furniture, chests for clothes and personal belongings, vessels for food and drink, lamps, oil for lamps—everything Zoser would want to make his afterlife as happy and as full as his life on earth.

To build Zoser's mastaba, ten thousand tons of limestone had been quarried from the plateau, and it had worked well. But the drab gray color did not please Imhotep. He wanted it to be a shining white—and not with plaster or whitewash. No! He would send crews across the Nile to the rock hills east of the river valley to cut the white limestone of Tura. So Tura limestone was brought to cover the entire mastaba.

Zoser's monument then stood gleaming white. But Imhotep was still not satisfied. He went to Zoser with a plan for enlarging it. Zoser accepted his idea and agreed to give him the workers he would need to build an extension that would add fourteen feet to each side of the mastaba and rise twenty-four feet high, or just two feet lower than the top of the original mastaba.

When the extension was completed, it gave the mastaba an exciting new dimension. The massive square now had a gigantic step on all four sides. But somehow, with the added step the square shape no longer pleased Imhotep. So he extended the structure by twenty-eight feet on the east end, making it rectangular in form.

While engrossed with developing his one-step mastaba, Imhotep had not neglected its underground complex. This too was being enlarged.

Imhotep had eleven shafts, each more than one hundred feet deep, dug down through the rock. At the end of each shaft a long gallery was built. Here, not far from Zoser's own burial chamber, were chambers for the members of his family.

In the meantime a tremendous amount of building was going on around the mastaba. Imhotep had not meant the tomb to stand alone. From the time he selected the site, he planned a beautiful grouping of buildings around the mastaba, including a temple, ceremonial chapels, connecting galleries, courtyards—all enclosed within a great white wall. And now that he knew how, everything was being constructed of stone.

Still, every time the architect looked at the great step, covered with Tura limestone, gleaming white in the sun, his imagination was fired. He visualized four more gigantic stone steps on top of the mastaba.

However, his construction so far consisted of stone laid in horizontal layers. This construction had been satisfactory for the original mastaba and the extensions. But Imhotep suspected that four immense squares, one on top of the other and weighing thousands of tons, might cause the building to collapse of its own weight.

He felt sure that there must be some way of laying the stone so the weight could be supported.

His solution was to build above the mastaba a series of independent walls leaning one against the other, rising steeply and sloping inward at an angle of about 75 degrees.

As the building rose higher under Imhotep's supervision, he was relieved to see that the construction method he had devised was sound. When the fourth step was finished, the great structure stood solid and firm.

Once more success fired his ambitions. He wanted to take his pyramid two steps higher.

By now Imhotep knew well how to organize the

many workers for maximum production. He also had learned to take advantage of seasonal labor. Most Egyptians were farmers. Their work periods depended on the seasonal flooding of the Nile. During these floods the farmers were idle. Imhotep put them to work.

The tools the workmen used were the same as in the past: hand tools of stone and copper. But the men using them functioned in a new way under Imhotep. They worked in teams.

The men were proud of their work groups. They chose names that they painted, bragging, on stones: the Vigorous Group, the Step Pyramid Group, the Enduring Gang. Working in organized teams, they could build as no men in the world had ever built before.

Once more Imhotep went to Zoser. He showed the pharaoh his plans for adding a fifth and sixth step to the pyramid, which would require a work force of several thousand more men. Zoser granted the request.

With these final steps added, the pyramid rose to a shining height of 204 feet and was the focal point of the most magnificent cluster of buildings ever seen by man. For Zoser's architect was not only a great builder, he was a bold and innovative designer.

No one before him had ever built a stone column. Imhotep designed tall white columns to heighten the splendor and drama of the whole complex. Many of the columns were carved with vertical flutings or grooves for a ribbed effect that caught and reflected the

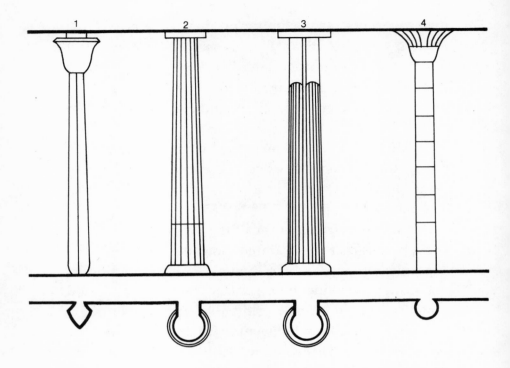

Fig. 3. Four of Imhotep's column designs. (1) This column represented the papyrus flower, the symbol of Lower Egypt. (2) Ribbed column. (3) Fluted column. (4) This represented the lotus blossom, symbol of Upper Egypt.

light. The tops of the columns were decorated with fine stone carvings of leaves, papyrus blossoms, and lotus flowers.

These columns were not used as supports—walls

served that purpose. For not even Imhotep yet knew how much weight a stone column could sustain. They were "engaged" columns, attached to the walls for added interest and elegance.

All the buildings were covered, like the pyramid, with white Tura limestone. A magnificent wall, more than thirty feet high, enclosed the whole area. Its four sides measured more than a mile in length and the lines of the wall were broken with handsome bays, some carved to resemble gateways.

But there was only one entrance into the enclosure. Guarded by tall twin towers, a narrow passageway led into a long, spacious arcade, its walls resplendent with forty-eight white limestone columns arranged in pairs, leading into the pyramid's courtyard.

Boatmen on the Nile saw the white pyramid shining in the sun long before they reached Memphis. From the capital city below and in the little mud villages and farms of the Nile valley, thousands gazed at the white splendor with pride and exultation. Many of them had helped build it. No one had ever seen a pyramid before. No one before them had ever dared build in stone. And only they knew how!

Zoser's reign was a time of achievement and progress. Not only was he a wise and able ruler, but he had Imhotep at his side. For early in his reign Zoser had also appointed Imhotep vizier, second only to the king in power, and his chief adviser. Together they made a brilliant team.

Zoser's Step Pyramid at Saqqara.

During his rule, Zoser was hailed by his people as a great and beloved monarch. Long after the pharaoh's death visitors to the pyramid and its necropolis wrote graffiti on the walls: "Zoser—Builder in Stone."

And what of Imhotep? Strangely enough, in his own time and for centuries after, his fame rested not on his genius as a builder but as a physician. His medical knowledge was enormous. A medical text written in his lifetime and attributed to him details 250 different kinds of diseases and prescribes methods for examin-

32

ing and diagnosing illnesses, some of them still used today.

But beyond this, his success in healing the sick was so great that people believed he possessed some supernatural power. During his lifetime and for long after, temples were built to him—sacred places where the sick and lame were thought to be magically cured by the spirit of Imhotep as they slept. Two thousand years after his death the Greeks, too, considered him a god and identified him with their own god of healing, Aesculapius.

Today Imhotep is remembered for his genius as a builder. And somewhere Imhotep the builder must have prepared for himself a magnificent tomb, richly furnished, elegantly appointed.

But no trace of his tomb has yet been discovered. If found intact, surely it would yield treasure beyond belief!

And Zoser? Was he buried in the handsome pink granite chamber deep below his white Step Pyramid? It is believed so.

2
The Plundering of the First Pyramid

For several hundred years Zoser's pyramid and the splendid structures around it stood as Imhotep had built them.

Then came a period in Memphis when the power of the pharaoh weakened. A monarch wanting to build to his own glory on the west plateau at Saqqara found it more practical to "borrow" stones from the Step Pyramid than to raise a large work force to cut them and haul them from the quarries. The white Tura limestone was highly desirable. "Borrowing" the stones started on a small scale. But as the centuries went on, plundering of the pyramid and its necropolis became the habit for anybody wanting stone for a building.

The predators were ruthless. Everything in their

way, anything they didn't want—statues, the small chapels, the decorative columns Imhotep had designed—was knocked down or destroyed.

Nor were the chambers and corridors beneath the pyramid safe. They too were stripped and pillaged of their riches by tomb robbers.

Imhotep had been so certain his pharaoh would be safe forever in the pink granite burial chamber hidden deep down in the rock. But robbers got in. The great stone stopper was wrenched from its hole, and the king's mummy stolen for the wealth of gold and jewels that lay between its wrappings. Managing the theft probably took cunning, bribery of the tomb guards, brutally hard work, and time.

The robbery may have taken place not long after Zoser's burial. In any case it was only the beginning of devastation. Over the centuries robbers emptied all the underground chambers of their furnishings and treasures. From the four great galleries that held Zoser's priceless belongings—golden objects studded with jewels, furniture sheathed in gold, carved chests filled with royal raiment—the tomb robbers took everything.

The burial chambers for his family, with the eleven richly furnished corridors, fared the same. The mummies were robbed and destroyed; all the treasures were stolen.

Stripped of everything of value, Zoser's pyramid was no longer of any interest to thieves and vandals.

In the nineteenth century a few individuals who

Fig. 4. Zoser's Step Pyramid and necropolis. The wall enclosing it was over 30 feet high; the length of its four sides measured more than a mile. (Artist's drawing after J-P. Lauer, la Pyramide à degrés, Vol. II, Plate IV)

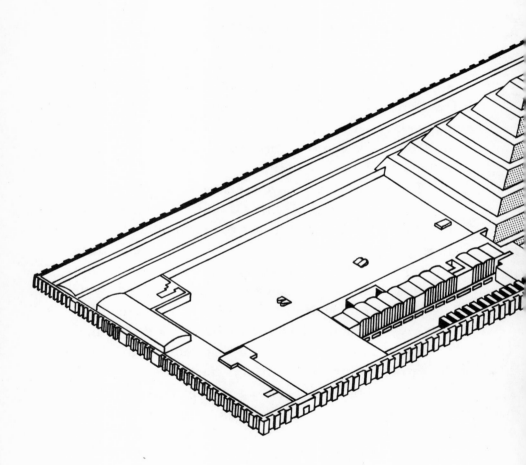

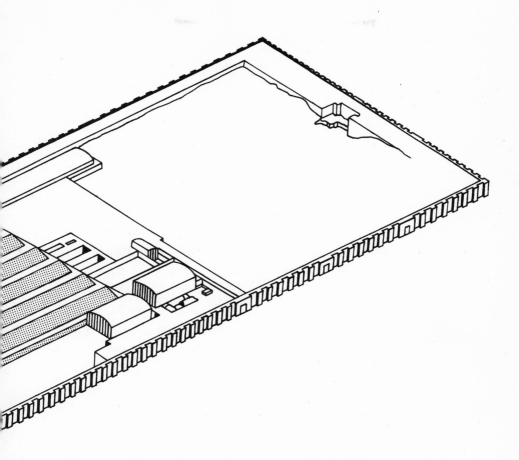

were interested in ancient Egypt found their way into the Step Pyramid. A British civil engineer, J. S. Perring, came upon a passageway containing sixty well-preserved mummies and thought he had found a communal tomb of Zoser's servants and retainers. However, examination of their wrappings showed that the mummies dated from a much later period. People who had lived and died almost two thousand years after Zoser had used his tomb as a convenient place for their own burials.

Some nineteenth-century explorers found things worth taking for foreign collections. Richard Lepsius, a German Egyptologist, came upon two small rooms decorated with blue tiles and connected by a carved doorway. He removed the doorway and some of the tiles to take back to the Berlin Museum.

But not until the beginning of the twentieth century was the Step Pyramid, both inside and outside, scientifically investigated by archeologists. These people were scholars interested in scientific investigation and painstaking restoration.

Making their way down to Zoser's burial chamber, they first saw the granite stopper lying on the roof of the chamber, beside the black hole it had once plugged. They flashed their electric torches down into the chamber. But the beam of light, playing back and forth, piercing the darkness, revealed nothing.

They lowered themselves through the hole into the burial chamber to make a minute examination.

Back in the dust and darkness they discovered a leg bone, still partly wrapped in ancient bandages. They believed it was Zoser's, wrenched off when tomb robbers, working in haste by the faint light of flickering torches, had pulled the mummy out of its coffin, then hurriedly hoisted it up through the unplugged hole to be carried away.

Searching the galleries of rooms surrounding

Zoser's burial chamber, the archeologists found nothing but a number of vases and vessels exquisitely carved from alabaster, crystal, and serpentine. Though cracked and broken, their original beauty was apparent, and eventually it would be restored. Only the contents of the vessels had been stolen—especially the oil. For in Ancient Egypt, oil was used as money.

When the archeologists entered the eleven corridors that contained the tomb chambers of the royal family, they hoped to uncover some proof of a royal burial—maybe even a mummy.

They found no mummy. But they did find evidence that burials had taken place—two fine alabaster coffins on limestone pedestals. One coffin was empty. The other held the skeleton of a small child. The child's coffin had a removable lining, which was made of six thin layers of beautifully grained wood, held together with small carved pegs. The archeologists found some tiny gold rivets in the innermost layer, indicating that the wood lining originally had been overlaid with sheets of gold that the robbers had stripped off.

Other pedestals, identical to the two that supported the alabaster coffins, were found in the chambers. The archeologists guessed that Zoser's family had been buried there, in the tombs prepared for them. But only the pedestals remained.

After the stone "borrowers" had stripped the Step Pyramid of its white Tura limestone cover and plundered its necropolis, the desert gradually took over.

The desert, always in motion, shifting with the winds, century after century, covered the ruins that surrounded the Step Pyramid and encroached on the pyramid itself.

Thus, when the archeologists came early in the twentieth century to study it, all they could see was the pyramid, standing alone. But when they dug beneath the deep accumulation of sand they began to uncover what remained of the splendid complex that once surrounded Zoser's pyramid.

Sometimes a find was baffling. Removing the sand at the southern end of the enclosure, the archeologists found a large stone mastaba. Beneath it a steep, sloping shaft, more than one hundred feet deep, led down through the rock to a small chamber. The room was a miniature replica of Zoser's own burial chamber—built of the same pink granite, with a room above it and a granite stone stopper to plug the roof hole. But the tomb chamber, which was empty, was too small to hold a body and the ceiling opening too small to admit one.

What had it been used for before the robbers emptied it? Surely something important to Zoser, for a lot of work and planning had gone into its building. Some archeologists think it might have held a casket containing the king's vital organs. Others recall that there was a belief in ancient Egypt that a pharaoh was always born with a stillborn twin, a brother who passed immediately into the beyond and who was symbolized by the placenta, or afterbirth. Had the placenta been preserved at Zoser's birth and buried in the small tomb when Zoser died?

Sometimes a find among the ruins seemed to have survived only by a miracle. Hundreds of fragments of smashed statues were uncovered, but one was found intact. It was a seated figure of Zoser, the only image of the pharaoh we have.

Today much of the grandeur and beauty that once surrounded the Step Pyramid lies buried. But archeologists are slowly rescuing and rebuilding some of its lost magnificence. Now the pyramid no longer stands alone. It looks down on a corner of the great Tura limestone enclosure wall, with its portal and colonnade. The wall, once more gleaming white in the sun, is so high it dwarfs a man standing beside it.

This was Egypt's first pyramid and many more would follow. But not one would have such a magnificent array of edifices surrounding it as Zoser's Step Pyramid had.

By building it, Zoser and Imhotep had ushered in a new era. The Pyramid Age had begun.

The earliest pyramids following Zoser's were step pyramids. Then came the transition toward what we think of as the true pyramid, with four smooth, sloping, triangular sides rising from a square base and meeting at an apex.

Only one hundred years after Zoser, the Pyramid Age reached its zenith.

The great enclosure wall of the Step Pyramid, which has been partially re-stored. The man at lower left is standing in the entrance.

42

This was achieved when Cheops built his Great Pyramid at Giza—the most magnificent of them all, not only in size but in workmanship.

Later Cheops's son, Chephren, built his own pyramid near his father's, a slightly smaller one. Cleverly set on a rise of ground, it looked as large, but it was not quite so fine in workmanship. When Chephren's successor, Mycerinus, inherited the throne, he built a still smaller one, nearby on the same plateau.

For almost five thousand years this group of three pyramids, rising from the desert, has been a wondrous, awe-inspiring sight. From Cairo, ten miles away, on a windless day when no sand clouds the air, they can be seen clearly silhouetted against the blue-silk sky.

Egypt's pharaohs continued to build pyramids for hundreds of years after the three pyramids of Giza were finished. But they became less and less important, smaller in size and increasingly inferior in workmanship.

Today there are at least eighty pyramids scattered along the west bank of the Nile. More may be found, hidden under tons of shifting sand. In 1951 the remains of a step pyramid were found not far from Zoser's, buried beneath the desert.

Some of those we see today are in ruins, though still recognizable as pyramids. Others rise in splendor toward the sun, giant, solitary monuments. But none impresses the beholder like Cheops's Great Pyramid of Giza. Rising in perfect symmetry, 481 feet high, its size alone is an enigma.

The Great Pyramid of Cheops. It is the only one of the original Seven Wonders of the Ancient World that still stands.

And this

The only tools to be had when it was built were simple hand tools; cutting edges were made from copper or sharpened stone. The wheel had not been invented, nor had the pulley. There were no beasts of burden. The pyramid was built entirely by the hands of men.

How did they manage it?

3
Why Were the Pyramids Built?

For all these thousands of years men have looked upon the pyramids of Egypt with awe and wonder. Cheops's Great Pyramid at Giza, the largest of the pyramids, covers an area of thirteen acres and is as tall as a forty-story building. And while more than two million great blocks of stone make up its mass, it is flawlessly constructed. The ancient Egyptians knew how to build their pyramids, whatever their size. Stone on stone, each stone cut precisely, fitted firmly in place, the structure rose solid and high. The pyramid was meant to last forever.

Centuries after the builders were gone, men asked: Why were these colossal structures built? What was the purpose of a pyramid?

The ancient Egyptian knew the answer: It was the home everlasting for his king, his pharaoh's Castle of Eternity.

But people of different times and different lands did not believe this. They thought it impossible that such an incredible construction would be built as a tomb—a tomb for *one* man.

They made guesses. The pyramids were built as repositories for priceless scientific data and relics; they were observatories for astronomers; they were great granaries used to store crops for lean years. . . .

And they were all wrong. They had looked at the pyramids, but they had not looked carefully at the people who built them.

From the simplest farmer and his wife to the pharaoh and his queen, the people of ancient Egypt had one strong, common bond—their belief in the continuation of life after death. The legend of their beloved god Osiris told them there was life after death. Osiris, a great and benevolent king on earth, was murdered by his jealous brother, Set, who tore the body into sixteen pieces and scattered them over Egypt. Osiris's wife, Isis, was grief-stricken. She managed with great difficulty to collect the pieces and bind them back together with strips of linen cloth. Then Anubis, god of the Netherworld, helped her with his magic spells. Life was breathed back into Osiris's body. Osiris could not return as a man to earth, but he triumphantly entered the Afterworld to live as a god and rule the region of the dead.

46

A statue of the goddess Isis, wife of Osiris. Here she is nursing her son Horus.

Osiris was a divine proof for the people of a continuance of life in the Afterworld. To be assured of life after death, however, there was one condition: the body had to be preserved.

This practice was rooted in a religious belief that within each person's body dwelled his *Ka*, a kind of spiritual "twin," or life-giving force. At death, the Ka left the body. But if the body was preserved, the Ka could return to it, restoring life to be lived in the Afterworld.

While the surest guarantee for a second life was preservation of the body, the ancient Egyptian took additional precautions to safeguard his identity. Statues of the dead man or woman were placed in the tomb; pictures showing the person's life on earth were drawn on the walls; his name was written over and over on objects in the tomb. But these were safeguards. The most important thing was to preserve the body in as lifelike a state as possible.

The Egyptians knew bodies could be kept lifelike long after death. They had found bodies buried in the dry, sterile sand, preserved by the hot, arid climate of their desert land. So it could be done. But how?

The ancient Egyptians found the answer. By thoroughly drying out the body, then wrapping it so it would stay dry, they could preserve it.

The day a person died, the body was taken by a procession of mourning family members and friends to the House of Embalming. This was usually an open-air tent that could be moved easily as needed.

Early the next morning the priests and workers arrived to begin the process of mummification. It would take about ten weeks.

The body, freshly bathed, was laid out on a long table, high enough so that the administering priests did not have to bend over. Beneath the table stood four jars called *canopic jars.* Later they would hold the embalmed organs of the corpse.

The priests were all clean-shaven: their heads, their faces, their bodies. They wore crisp white linen robes. The priest in charge of the embalming rituals wore a jackal-head mask. He represented the god Anubis, guardian of the tombs, who had the body of a man and the head of a jackal.

Led by the priest in the jackal mask, the priests intoned religious chants signaling that the first step toward mummification was about to begin. This was the removal of the brain, an operation performed by a highly skilled specialist.

First, he slipped a long, slender, hooklike instrument up one nostril and, working in a circular movement, he broke through the ethmoid bone into the brain cavity. Then withdrawing the hooked tool, he substituted a long, spirally twisted rod with a small, spoon-shaped tip. He reached into the cranial cavity with the rod and began to draw out the brain, bit by bit, until he was sure the cavity was clear and clean. If the delicate job was completed successfully, the face wouldn't be marred or disfigured.

Next the nostrils were cleaned and plugged with

wax, then the mouth was washed out. The face was bathed and coated with a resinous paste. A small piece of linen was placed over each eyeball and the eyelids drawn over the cloth.

The body was then ready for the second important operation—removal of the viscera from the body cavity. The Egyptians had learned that if the brain and the viscera were left in the body, they would deteriorate rapidly, making the drying-out process and successful mummification impossible.

The specialist who did this job held a flat, black stone, one side of which was filed to razor sharpness. The priest in the jackal mask turned the body slightly on its right side, dipped a rush pen in ink, and drew a spindle-shaped line about five inches long down the left side. Following the line, the man with the stone cut a deep incision, then reached in and severed and removed each organ: liver, stomach, kidneys, lungs, intestines. Only the heart, believed to be the seat of intelligence and feeling, had to be left intact within the body. The organs he removed were wrapped in resin-soaked cloth and placed in the canopic jars to await burial with the mummy.

The body cavity was cleansed, the incision pulled together and closed with a seal bearing an all-powerful symbol: the Eye of Horus.

Thin wires were fastened around each fingernail and toenail. The corpse was bathed once more. The body was ready to be dried out.

It was lifted from the high table and placed on a

mat woven of plant fibers, then covered with a powder called *natron*, which came from the Libyan desert. A good drying agent, natron was thought to have purifying powers as well. Day after day, with the help of the hot, dry climate, the body finally became wholly dry. Stretched on its frame of bone, it still retained the shape and features of the person who had died.

For the last time the body was bathed, anointed with fragrant oils, and rubbed with sweet-smelling spices and herbs. The priests poured out libations to restore moisture symbolically to the body. They burned incense to give it back its warmth.

The body was ready to be wrapped.

About 150 yards of cloth, torn into strips of various widths, were used. On some strips the corpse's name was written. Others bore the figures of the gods, magic formulas, or religious supplications.

The bandaging started with the limbs: the legs first, then the arms. The torso was next, and finally the head. The process was intricate and required skill. And because it was fraught with religious significance it could not be hurried.

Throughout the wrapping the priests were there to perform their rituals. They indicated where the magical bandages should be placed, and where charms and amulets should be hidden among the wrappings.

When the wrapping was completed, the mummy was brought back to the House of Mourning. Usually about seventy days had elapsed since death.

The successfully mummified body would last for-

51

ever if it was protected, its wrappings left undisturbed. Thus, to the ancient Egyptian, the tomb where the mummy would "live" was of great concern and importance. The tomb was not thought of as a receptacle for the dead—far from it. It was known as the "House of Eternity." And a pharaoh's tomb was called the "Castle of Eternity."

The Egyptians believed the Afterworld was a kind of Utopia, life on earth idealized. Pictures on tomb walls depicting the Afterworld show crops more lush than anything known on earth, streams full of fish, vines heavy with fruit. Plump game abounds in the forests. All the worldly pleasures are enjoyed—hunting, fishing, music, dancing, eating, drinking. In the Afterworld people could, if they wished, continue their vocations. The pharaoh, now a god, still ruled, and his aides attended him. The farmer could reap rich crops without effort. The scribe happily filled rolls of papyrus with his writings.

In order to enjoy all these activities, the person would need the same things he or she had required on earth. These objects were placed in the tomb with the mummy at the time of burial.

For a poor man or woman, the needs would be simple and the tomb small. But as a man's wealth increased, his need for material things grew too. And for a person of high rank, especially a pharaoh or a queen, the tomb was lavishly furnished and supplied so that life could continue in the Afterworld on the same grand scale as on earth.

King Cheops. This two-inch ivory statue was found in Abydos.

The tomb was the Egyptian's house after death. There his mummy and personal belongings would be safely sheltered forever.

The greatest of these tombs were the pyramids.

4
Building the Great Pyramid

Traffic on the Nile was always heavy. But it was never so heavy as when workmen in hundreds of boats sailed to Giza to help build a pyramid for their young pharaoh, Cheops.

On their way they passed all the pyramids built by earlier pharaohs. Zoser's Step Pyramid, the first one built, was now almost a hundred years old. And the two most recent ones had been erected by Cheops's father, the pharaoh Seneferu.

Seneferu's Bent Pyramid, built early in his reign, was bow-shaped, because a crack had developed in the interior of the structure when it was half its intended height, and the angle had been changed. Nevertheless, it was impressive in its bulk and well constructed. Just

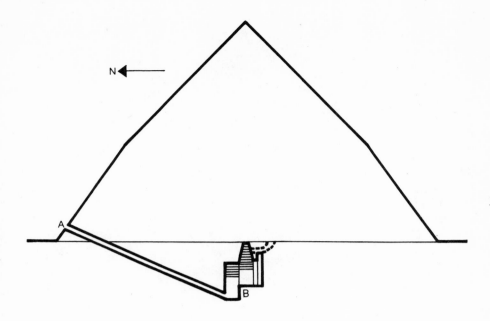

Fig. 5. The only pyramid with more than one entrance is Seneferu's Bent Pyramid. All the pyramids have an entrance on the north face; Seneferu's has an additional one on the west. The north entrance (Top, A) tunnels down 240 feet into the rock below the pyramid to a large room (B) with a remarkable corbelled ceiling soaring 57 feet high. The west entrance (Bottom, A) descends 211 feet through the pyramid's core to ground level, where it flattens out for another 66 feet. There it enters a high-ceilinged room that lies above and southeast of the room reached by the northern entrance. These chambers are not connected, and archeologists found both to be empty.

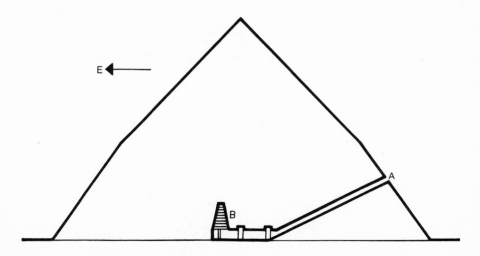

The Bent Pyramid, built by the pharaoh Seneferu, rises from the desert on the west bank of the Nile at Dashur, south of Saqqara. When the pyramid had reached a little more than half its present height, the angle of its slope was abruptly changed from 54 degrees to 43 degrees, and its bowed shape resulted. Probably the best preserved of all the pyramids, it still retains part of its Tura limestone casing. Seneferu may have been disappointed in his pyramid's appearance, since he later built a second pyramid nearby: the Northern Pyramid. That rises 300 feet in perfect pyramid form, and is considered Egypt's first true pyramid.

north of it was Seneferu's second pyramid. Larger than all the others, it was the first pyramid to reach a great height while achieving the true pyramid form.

Cheops, inspired by his father's success, would build on a still larger scale.

The site chosen by Cheops for his pyramid lay on the west bank of the Nile, north of all the other pyramids, at Giza. There, beneath the desert sand, was an immense plateau of solid limestone, an expanse more than large enough to build the biggest pyramid ever and a great complex of buildings that would surround it.

As soon as the site was chosen, workmen began clearing the square area where the pyramid would stand. Under a blazing sun they worked, naked except for a folded loincloth, scooping the sand into baskets that they carried as far as half a mile away to dump in the desert. Back and forth they moved, back and forth.

The square base of the pyramid would cover an area of thirteen acres. The length of each of the four sides had to be accurately measured. The Egyptians had measuring devices, including wooden rods and chalk lines, which were skillfully woven of strands of flax so that they would not stretch.

But to measure perimeters of this great length, another device was more practical. The circumference of a log was measured. When the log was rolled, a notch marked each complete turn until the desired distance was recorded. Each turn introduced the mathematical function of π into the measurement. Probably the pyramid builders did not know that the circumference of a circle is equal to twice its diameter multiplied by π ($2D \times 3.1416$). But more than four thousand years later, scientists marveled at how often they found the ratio of

π appearing in the ancient Egyptain calculations.

When every inch of the thirteen-acre square was cleared of sand, down to bedrock, the rough surfaces of the rock base were evened and smoothed.

Next the builders were faced with the problem of making sure the site was level. For if the pyramid were to rise, high and true, and last forever—as Cheops intended it should—each of the four sides of the base had to be on a precisely level plane.

The perimeter of the area to be leveled was immense—each side was more than 755 feet long—and the small wooden levels used by carpenters were of course useless.

But the builders knew a simple method. The surface of standing water was always level. The people of Egypt through the ages had depended on the River Nile for their very existence. Their irrigation systems alone had made them experts in the ways and uses of water. It was quite natural to employ water as their tool for leveling the pyramid site precisely.

Workmen hauled mud from the Nile up to the site and a low mud wall was built around the four sides of the square. Then the enclosure was filled with water. Shallow trenches were cut into the rock, all at the same depth beneath the water's surface, and the water level marked on the sides of the trenches. When the area was drained, the builders could see exactly where the rock had to be cut and evened to give them a precise level for their building.

Now they had to make sure that the pyramid was a perfect square with each side oriented exactly to the four cardinal points—North, South, East, and West.

The first step was to establish a true and exact North. This was done by observing and measuring the rising and setting of a star. A ritual priest who was an

Fig. 6. Sighting on the stars to establish true north, an early exercise in astronomy.

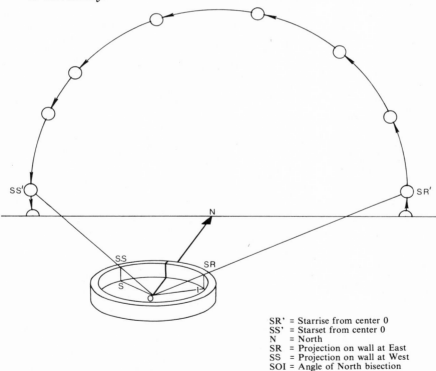

SR' = Starrise from center 0
SS' = Starset from center 0
N   = North
SR = Projection on wall at East
SS = Projection on wall at West
SOI = Angle of North bisection

astronomer did this job. A small circular wall was built on the leveled site, high enough so that the priest standing within the circle could see nothing but the sky. Facing East, he watched for a specific star to rise. The instant he saw the star he marked the spot on the wall that the star seemed to rise from, then drew a line from that mark to the center of the circle. He waited for the star to move in its arc across the sky, and when it set in the west he drew another line that met the first in the center of the circle. By drawing another perpendicular line at the midpoint he got an accurate North-South line and a reading of true North. The priest repeated his observations with several other stars before having the circular wall removed.

While the site was being readied, barracks were built nearby to house a permanent work force. Four thousand or more men would live there all year round: engineers, designers, architects, master masons, surveyors, toolmakers.

As these men moved onto the site, crews of quarrymen were cutting stones for the pyramid: the gray limestone on the Giza plateau, the fine white limestone from across the river at Tura, and the splendid colored granites—brown, black, deep red, and pink—quarried 590 miles up the Nile at Aswan.

Since Imhotep first pioneered building with stone, workmen had become more adept at quarrying the big blocks. Using copper chisels and wooden mallets and wedges, they could cut blocks to specified shapes and sizes with remarkable skill. While none of it was easy, cutting the stone from the outcrops at Giza was not too difficult. But across the river, at Tura, the workmen had to tunnel deep into the hills for the stone, often far below the surface.

And far up the Nile, the hard Aswan granite was brutal to quarry. But the men were skilled. Using abrasives and sharp tools, they laboriously cut slots into the stone and inserted wooden wedges. When water was poured onto the wedges, they would swell and split the granite along fairly straight planes.

After the stone was cut, there came the crucial undertaking of getting the blocks from the quarries to the pyramid site. This prodigious task would have been impossible without the annual flooding of the Nile. In flood, the river grew wider and wider, spreading closer and closer to the pyramid site until the Nile's west bank was only a quarter of a mile from the plateau. Then stones that came by boat—the limestone from Tura and granite from Aswan—could be sailed within a short distance of the work site.

Moreover, only when the Nile was in flood were there thousands and thousands of farmers available for the enormous job of getting the stones to the pyramid site. From mid-July until late October, when their land was under water, the idle farmers could be put to work hauling stone, just as they had in Imhotep's time a century earlier.

The limestone blocks quarried in Giza were

loaded on sledges and hauled overland to the pyramid site. It was backbreaking work. The men, working in teams, strained at the pull ropes, their bodies wet with sweat and sticky with sand. Sometimes a man dropped, and the whole team faltered. But he was quickly replaced, or the others labored on without him.

From Tura, the white limestone, roped onto sledges, was pulled from the inland quarries to the east bank of the Nile. There the stones—the smallest weighing two tons—were loaded on barges. Built of tightly woven reed, the barges were strong but light and maneuverable. The stones were ferried five miles down and across the swollen river, through strong currents, to the west bank landing area. It was a rough haul on land, and a dangerous boat trip.

But bringing the granite blocks from the quarries at Aswan was the most formidable feat. These were massive stones. Some, including the slabs needed for the king's burial chamber, weighed as much as fifty tons. After they were hauled to the water's edge and loaded onto reed barges, only the most expert and fearless boatmen could bring them the 590 miles down the fast-flowing river. Navigating the Nile in flood was tricky, and the stretches of shifting sand banks were treacherous. When these boats reached the landing area at Giza, shouts of victory and welcome rose in the air!

Whether the stones came from Aswan or Tura, there was still the terrible job of hauling them from the river bank to the top of the plateau.

For this purpose a steep stone road, a causeway, had been built from the river up to the plateau's summit. The stones would be hauled up this incline on sledges by the only beasts of burden known: men.

At the foot of the causeway large teams of men harnessed together waited until the stone was securely lashed onto a sledge and the sledge fastened to their draw ropes. If a man lifted his eyes and saw the steep road sloping up, the summit looked far away. Actually, it was about 225 feet to the top. But men pulling a sledge with a stone weighing fifty tons or more found it was a long, hard climb.

They could make it only by working in unison. They learned to pull to a kind of chanted rhythm: *Ahhhhhhh*—PULL ... *Ahhhhhhh*—PULL .... With every man surging forward at once, the combined pulling force was powerful. A man standing on the front of the sledge poured liquid under the sledge runners to lessen the friction against the paving stone. That was the only help they had.

When they reached the top, men using ropes and stout wooden poles as levers moved the stones from the sledges and turned them over to masons for trimming and smoothing.

The design for the stone mass of the pyramid called for three parts, each making its own demands on the stonemasons' skills.

By far the most numerous were the core stones that would form the bulk of the pyramid's interior. While these were accurately cut to specification, only

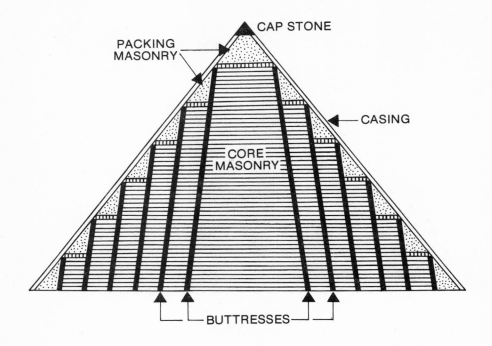

Fig. 7. To strengthen a pyramid, the ancient Egyptian architects, starting with Imhotep, built a series of ascending limestone buttresses. These "ribs" were laid up at a steeper angle (about 75 degrees) than the pyramid's final Tura limestone casing (about 52 degrees), and stabilized the rough-hewn core stones that formed the bulk of the structure. It is assumed that all the pyramids were built this way, but only those damaged or left unfinished can be examined.

the blocks on the outermost layer of each tier had to be smoothly finished, or dressed, on all sides. The other stones were dressed only on the bottom surfaces, so they would sit firm and level. Some roughness where they joined on the sides was unimportant.

But the blocks to be placed next to these, the packing stones, had to fit smoothly, snugly together and were carefully finished on all surfaces. These would protect the core stones and fill the spaces or "steps" that would be created by placing successively smaller squares atop each other as the pyramid rose, tier on tier.

Next to the packing stones, and forming the outside cover of the pyramid, would be the casing stones of Tura limestone. These stones, covering the entire surface, would give the finished pyramid its smooth surface and white magnificence. And it required the skill of the finest stonemasons to trim and dress them. Thousands of years later, scientists marveled at the "optician's precision" with which these blocks were cut to fit.

More than six million tons of stone would be hauled to the site before the pyramid was finished. For while there would be a little open space inside the pyramid, including a handsome burial chamber for the king, most of the structure's great bulk would be solid stone. And most of the hundred thousand men working in any given year would be working with stone. Among the most highly skilled of these were the masons.

Stones weighing up to ten tons were so finely, so precisely cut and trimmed by the masons that the space between them measured less than one-fiftieth of an inch. And a film of mortar wiped on their surfaces as a lubricant when the blocks were slid into place dried to a line as fine as a hair.

The architects' design called for the cover of Tura limestone to rest on a solid pavement. So the first step in building the pyramid was to lay a wide strip of Tura limestone around the entire perimeter of the thirteen-acre site.

Then the pyramid began to rise.

The first tier, or course, and even the second, could be done from the ground. But as the pyramid grew, and thousands and thousands of blocks were needed for each tier, a ramp system was used. The ramps were built of stone rubble held together with Nile mud. Men pulled the blocks, loaded on sledges, up the ramp to the course that was being built, stone by stone, tier by tier.

The interior chambers and most of the passage-ways were built in as the courses were laid. There would be 201 courses, or tiers, from base to capstone when the pyramid reached its full height of 481 feet.

Cheops's pyramid took at least twenty years to finish. The work of a million people, perhaps more, had gone into its construction. Some had lost their lives, for the work was dangerous, with the lifting and shifting of monolithic stones, the brutal heat, the flooding of the Nile. But all the others, from the genius designers who had drawn the plans to the laborers who had hauled the stones, knew with pride that it was their talent, skill, and toil that had produced this magnificent monument to their king.

Though thousands of separate blocks made up its white cover, the surface was smooth and shining. As if by some magic, the white mantle seemed to be placed on each of the four sides in one giant sheath. On the very top, the towering capstone pointed to the sky.

Like the pyramids of Zoser and other pharaohs, Cheops's pyramid did not stand alone. It dominated a necropolis of magnificent buildings, including three small pyramids, one of them the tomb for the pharaoh's favorite queen.

The necropolis was called the Great City of the Dead. But most of the living who came there did not come to mourn. They came by boat, all through the day, starting at dawn when the first rays of the sun struck the white stone pyramid.

Their reasons were many. Some came on funeral barges to take part in rituals that would send their dead off on the journey to a happy second life. Others came with offerings for the gods or gifts for relatives now living in the Other World. Many came for the pure joy of being there.

As the people left their boats, some remembered an earlier time when reed barges, laden with stone, had pulled up there in the heat and mud. Then the causeway was rough and dusty, crowded with shouting laborers struggling to pull the stones to the top.

But all the toil and ugliness was in the past. Now there on the west bank of the Nile they saw the valley temples—serene, fragrant with incense—where rituals were performed for the dead. And the causeway leading up to the pyramid was paved and enclosed, with a roof and wall of Tura limestone. In its roof were horizontal slits through which the sun filtered, lighting up the interior and bringing to life the elegantly carved reliefs on the walls.

At the upper end of the causeway stood the mortuary temple with its surrounding cloisters. Just beyond, towering over all, rose Cheops's pyramid. In its shadow were the three smaller pyramids, each with its own chapel. And nearby stood the magnificent mastabas for the royal family and relatives. West of the pyramid were the wide avenues of mastabas, tombs for the nobles and officials who would attend Cheops after death as they had in life.

The City of the Dead was a joyous place, full of sound and life. The rhythmic chants of priests filled the air. The voices of the people—men, women, and children—rose and fell in greetings and praise. Over all lay the sweet fragrance of incense and scented oils.

By day the sun, shining on the great expanse of white limestone, bathed the necropolis in a shimmering light. And at night starlight and moonlight were reflected in the white mirror surfaces. The pyramid was never dark. It was always visible.

5
The Caliph's Story

Today the three Giza pyramids—Cheops's, Chephren's and Mycerinus's—stand stripped of their radiant white mantles. They are a beige monotone in color, though the monotone changes with the changing light of day and the moon at night. The only remnant of the shining white Tura limestone that once covered them is a small patch near the summit of Chephren's pyramid.

The splendid limestone was not destroyed by weather or natural disasters or war. It was lost to greed: most of it was stolen.

The first known assault on the Great Pyramid's white facade was in A.D. 820. It was made in a search for treasure by Abdullah al Mamun, a young Muslim

An aerial view of the Giza pyramids: Cheops's in the foreground,
Chephren's in the center, and Mycerinus in the background.

caliph, or leader. He was a son of Caliph Harun al-Rashid of *Arabian Nights* fame.

By that time Egypt had been the victim of several foreign invasions. It was under the rule of Arab conquerors who were followers of Mohammed.

The Caliph Mamun was a scholar as well as an adventurer. He had been informed that the Great Pyramid contained not only treasures beyond belief, but documents accurately charting the earth and heavens, information known only to the ancient Egyptians. Also hidden within the pyramid, it was said, were strange and magical objects, such as glass that could be bent without breaking and iron that would not rust.

Mamun arrived with a large crew of men, determined to find the pyramid's hidden entrance and reach its treasures.

The caliph had been advised that a pyramid's entrance was usually on the north side. So for days his men crawled around the northern face, slipping and sliding, trying to get small toeholds on the joints of the limestone casing. But they found no sign of an entrance. Then they turned their search to the other three sides. There too they found nothing but the smooth surface of stone.

The caliph would not give up. They would have to break their way in.

He chose a spot on the north side, seven courses, or tiers, up from the base of the pyramid. The area around the pyramid was littered with stone fragments and sand, which the caliph ordered heaped into a large

71

mound. When wetted down with water it hardened, making a firm base from which the men could operate. The caliph hoped that by great good luck they might hit the entrance, or at least break into an adjoining corridor that would take them into the pyramid.

The strongest men, using the heaviest hammers and sharpest chisels, began the job. They scarcely marred the stone. Chisels were blunted and resharpened. Men tired and were replaced. But they could not break the Tura limestone.

However, they knew of another way to crack stone: the alternate use of heat and cold. They built roaring fires on the sand against the stone face, and when the stone was blisteringly hot, splashed it with cold vinegar, repeating the process until the stone cracked. They then attacked with battering rams.

They hit no sealed entrance. Actually, they were boring right into the solid core of the pyramid. Progress was agonizingly slow. As they smashed in farther, heat and dust and lack of air in the confined space made work all but impossible.

They had gone one hundred feet and the caliph was ready to give up when suddenly they heard an awesome sound, a great thud, as if something heavy had fallen in the depths of the pyramid. Aiming their battering rams in the direction of the sound, they pushed on and broke into a small, dirty passage less than four feet high and a little more than a yard wide. On the floor was a stone slab their battering rams had dislodged from the low ceiling.

The passage slanted upward at a 26-degree angle. The men began crawling up. They had gone almost a hundred feet when the corridor ended in a stone wall. They had no way of knowing it, but the dead end of the wall of stone was the solidly sealed entrance they had searched for. If the caliph had aimed his battering rams seven tiers higher and a bit eastward they would have hit it.

They crawled back down to the fallen stone slab. Peering around it they saw that the passageway continued on down beyond it. Crouching and on hands and knees, they made their way down, a seemingly endless journey, for more than three hundred feet. Then the passage leveled off, becoming horizontal. A short distance after, it opened into a large unfinished chamber. The rock walls were rough hewn, the floors uneven, with great gaps where paving stones were missing. Obviously the chamber had never been finished, never used. On the walls the caliph saw faint smudges of smoke, left by the torches of much earlier visitors, probably Romans and Greeks long ago. If anything of interest or value had ever been in the room—which the caliph doubted—there was nothing left.

Disgusted, Mamun and his men crawled back up to where the slab of stone had fallen. They were ready to leave the pyramid through the opening they had made. But first they stopped to look at the stone and the black, empty place above it. Raising a torch they were amazed to see, not gray limestone, but an expanse of red-black granite. The fallen stone had been placed

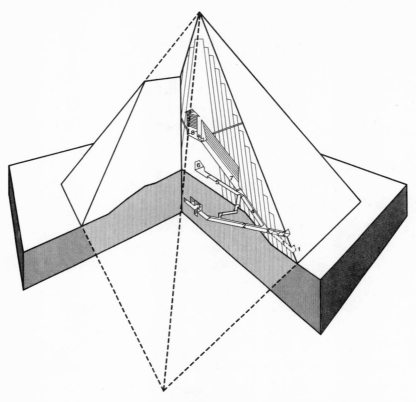

Fig. 8. The route of the Caliph Mamun and his men inside the Great Pyramid. The Caliph's men battered a hole into the pyramid (1, dotted line) and tunneled in, breaking into a low, upward-sloping passage (2), which ended in a stone wall (actually the pyramid's original sealed entrance). Going back down, they climbed over a large stone (X) that their battering rams had dislodged and continued down the passageway until it ended in an unfinished chamber (3). Crawling back up, they examined the hole left in the ceiling by the falling stone and saw that it opened into a narrow, ascending passage (4), which they found blocked by three large granite plugs and a series of limestone plugs. Negotiating the plugs, they entered a level passageway

there to hide it. The caliph wondered: Could it be a plug blocking an entrance to another corridor?

Climbing up to investigate, Mamun found a low, narrow passage completely blocked by a great granite plug. It stood solidly from floor to ceiling, and touched the walls on both sides so nobody could get through.

Now the caliph and his men were excited. Surely beyond the plug was the passageway that would lead them to treasure.

First they tried to dislodge the plug. But they soon realized the plug was too large, fitted so tightly it could not be moved.

Then they tried to smash it. This, too, was useless—their chisels and hammers bounced off it, scarcely scratching the surface.

If they could not move it or break it, there was only one other way. The caliph saw that the walls of the passage were gray limestone, not as hard as granite. He told his men to chop into the wall, cutting away space so they could pass around the plug.

It was not easy. There was little space in which to

———————

(5), which dead-ended in a large, square room (6), which the Caliph named the Queen's Chamber. Retracing their steps, they stopped where the level passageway and the ascending passage met to see if the latter might continue upward. It did, opening into a magnificent, high-ceilinged gallery (7) that sloped upward, leading to Cheops's burial chamber (8) and his empty sarcophagus.

work. They had to kneel, stooped over in choking dust.

When they finally cut away enough wall to bypass the plug, they found a second great plug right behind it. And next to that a third, all identical. By the time they bypassed the third plug they had excavated a passageway in the wall eighteen feet long.

Even now they were not finished with plugs! The corridor they crawled into proved to be blocked with a series of plugs. However, they were of limestone. It was possible to demolish them with hammers and chisels.

The last limestone plug dealt with, they found themselves in another low, narrow passageway that ascended steeply. They crawled up more than 120 feet before they hit a level spot. This was the beginning of another passage, still so low and narrow they were forced to crawl, but at least it was level.

Suddenly their flickering torches showed a drop in the floor, a "step" more than two feet deep. Now they could stand! They walked a short distance along the heightened passage, which then led into a room.

The room had a high, pointed ceiling. The caliph, not knowing that the pyramid was a tomb only for the pharaoh, misnamed it the Queen's Chamber, because Arab tombs were built with gabled ceilings for women and flat ceilings for men.

The room was almost square, about eighteen feet long and almost as wide. It was empty.

In one wall there was a niche which the men, hungry for treasure, thought might lead to another chamber. They pounded it and broke the stones. But there was no hollow sound, no sign of anything but solid masonry.

Again disappointed, they started back the way they had come. They followed the level corridor to where it joined the ascending corridor they had crawled up. But before crawling back down it, Mamun had an idea. Was it possible that the ascending corridor did not end at the level passage as they thought? Perhaps it continued upward, into the pyramid.

Investigating, they found it did. So they started up the low, narrow passage on their hands and knees. Almost at once it opened out into a great hall.

Rekindling their torches, holding them high, the caliph and his men found themselves in a different world! They were at the bottom of a magnificent inclined gallery of highly polished limestone. The white stone walls climbed to a ceiling so high the lights of their torches could not reach it.

They started up the steeply sloping floor, only to find that with each step forward they slipped back on the polished surface. Then they saw that on each side of the passage there was a low stone ramp, notched at intervals, which gave them better footing. They finally scrambled 153 feet up to the upper end of the gallery.

At the top of the gallery was a large rectangular block of stone. Climbing over it, the caliph's men were in another passageway so low they again had to crawl.

After a short distance the passage heightened and widened and became a kind of antechamber. Excitement grew as their torches showed them the walls here were of an entirely different stone—a rich, red-brown granite.

The caliph was jubilant. He knew that at last they were within steps of the burial chamber. There they would find not only the golden treasures buried with the king, but the ancient documents and magical objects he coveted.

They had one more short stretch of crawling through a low passage before they reached the doorway to the chamber.

They entered a handsome room, more than thirty feet long and half that wide, high ceilinged and built entirely of the polished dark red-brown granite. The caliph called it the King's Chamber. And this time he was right.

Near one wall stood a large granite sarcophagus. The caliph and his men rushed to it, sure of finding the pharaoh's mummy.

The sarcophagus was lidless. And it was empty.

Certain that somewhere within the room treasure must be hidden, the men began searching for concealed niches, a block of stone that might be moved to reveal a secret passage or chamber. They crawled over every inch of the floor and stood on each other's shoulders to hammer against the wall. But all was solid, smooth, tightly fitted granite. And when they held their torches high they saw that the flat ceiling was as smooth as the floor.

The men, in anger and frustration after all they had suffered to reach the burial chamber, hacked at the walls and the floor. Finally they left as they had come—empty-handed.

An Arab legend claims that Mamun later had a cache of gold hidden in the pyramid for his men to find, pacifying them somewhat and recompensing them for their labors.

Ironically, the scholar Mamun had not read the writings of the Greek scholar Strabo. If he had, he would have known the location of the pyramid's entrance. Strabo visited the pyramid in 24 B.C., more than eight hundred years before the caliph, and described the entrance in his *Geographica*. Strabo reported that a stone could be raised up, revealing a sloping passage into the pyramid. When dropped back into place, the stone fit so smoothly into the surrounding masonry it was impossible to detect it. This was at the seventeenth course on the northern face of the pyramid, seventy-one feet up and twenty-four feet east of the center. Mamun missed it by aiming his battering rams too low, at the tenth course and west of the center.

The opening he and his men battered into the side of the pyramid is there today. Since it is much closer to the ground, and thus more easily accessible than the original entrance, it is used by visitors entering the pyramid. It is still known to many as "Mamun's Hole."

The white casing of the Great Pyramid remained undisturbed for more than four hundred years after Mamun. Then in the thirteenth century its total destruction began.

The Arab rulers of Egypt were building a new capital city across the Nile, about five miles east of Giza. They called their city Al Kahira, "The Triumphant." We know it today as Cairo. Within its great white walls there would be splendid palaces for their sultans and, since the Arabs were Mohammedans, great mosques and minarets to the glory of their god, Allah.

To build Al Kahira required a lot of stone. And there, within sight, was the largest pile of quarried stone in the world: the Great Pyramid.

The Arabs began stripping the stone from the lower tiers where it was most accessible. And the first Tura limestone they tore off the Great Pyramid was used for bridges across the Nile over which camel trains would carry the thousands of tons of stone that would eventually be used.

Meantime, stripping of the other two pyramids had begun. First they stripped the lower tiers, then gradually worked their way up higher and higher as more stone was required.

Finally all three pyramids of Giza were completely stripped of their white limestone, except for the patch left near the summit of Chephren's.

It was a mammoth job. More than twenty-two acres of Tura limestone eight feet thick covered the

Great Pyramid alone. The smallest stones weighed at least two tons. Yet some archeologists believe it may have been done over a relatively short period of time—a hundred years, more or less.

While the shining white limestone is gone forever from Giza's pyramids, it is not all lost to sight. Some of the stone can be seen today in Cairo. Tura limestone from the Great Pyramid, for example, was used by the Arabs in the fourteenth century when they built their city's most magnificent mosque, the mosque of Sultan Hassan. After six hundred years the mosque still stands as the most celebrated piece of Arabic architecture in Egypt.

Several centuries after the sultan's mosque was built, a new kind of visitor came to the pyramids of Giza. These men came from Europe—Italy, Germany, France, many from England. They came not out of greed to seek treasure or to steal stones. They came out of curiosity—to explore. Especially intrigued with the mysteries of the Great Pyramid, some of them would bring to it a new sound—the roar of gunpowder.

6
Explorers and Gunpowder

When the explorers came from Europe to investigate the Great Pyramid they had no problem getting in. After the Arabs stripped off its Tura limestone cover, the pyramid's original entrance was plainly exposed. Four hundred years before that, Mamun, battering in his opening, had made the pyramid's interior easily accessible.

Opening the pyramid led to a strange and odious invasion: hordes of bats. The winged mammals found the Great Pyramid's dark passageways with their rough stone walls ideal for nesting and breeding. Through the centuries they grew in numbers and to enormous size. Their bodies measured a foot or more long and their wingspreads two feet.

If firearms brought by the Europeans could have

annihilated the bats, guns in the Great Pyramid might have made sense. But the bats were most troublesome in the low, narrow, stifling passageways where firing a gun was not advisable, as one of the early explorers learned.

An English mathematician, John Greaves, came to Giza in the 1630s to investigate and measure the Great Pyramid. He was "crawling like a serpent" down a corridor when he found himself in a swarm of huge bats and fired his gun to scare them away. Little harm was done to the bat population, but the heat and smoke, added to the fetid air, the showers of rubble, and the deafening roar, were hard on Greaves.

Luckily he survived to carry on his explorations and write about them. In fact, a discovery reported by Greaves was to baffle other explorers until it was solved more than a hundred years after he had gone.

At the lower end of the Grand Gallery, Greaves found an opening about three feet wide in the wall at floor level. He saw that a stone block that once covered the opening had been removed. Peering down, he saw a dark hole. Puzzled, Greaves climbed into the opening, and using the rough-cut sides as precarious foot- and handholds, he managed to get partway down. But stench, foul air, and swarms of bats drove him back. When he returned to England and wrote a pamphlet on his experiences, he recorded his discovery of the mysterious shaft, and his battle with the bats, including his attempt to fight them off with gunpowder.

Others who followed him limited their gunfire to

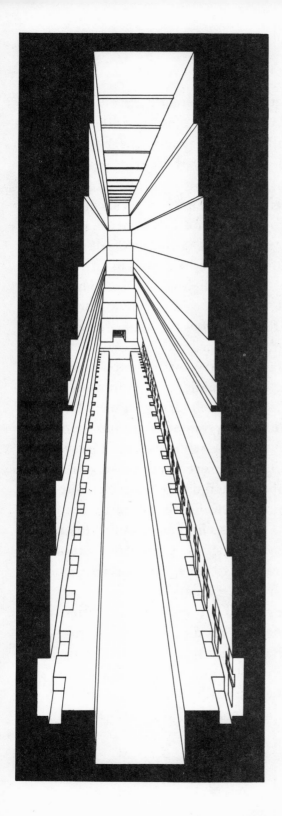

Fig. 9. The Grand Gallery in the Great Pyramid is the architectural marvel of the Pyramid Age. Built of polished limestone, and soaring to a height of 28 feet, it slopes upward at a 26 degree angle for a total length of 153 feet. Along each wall runs a ramp 2 feet high and 20 inches wide. The passage between the ramps is only 3 feet 5 inches wide. No one knows just why such a spendid, inclined gallery—accessible only through low, narrow, rough-cut passages—was built. Archeologists believe it was used as a storage place for the three granite plugs that, after Cheops's burial, were slid down into the ascending corridor (see Fig. 10, 3) to block access to the Pharaoh's tomb.

the entrance or just beyond so they could retreat quickly until the blasts' havoc subsided. Mostly they fired out of unfounded fear. Some fired to frighten off serpents—though there were no snakes in the pyramid. Some blasted away to scare off "evil spirits." An English adventurer named George Sandys arrived at the pyramid's entrance with a bodyguard of native soldiers in the seventeenth century. He wrote in his journal that he ordered his men to fire their harquebuses in the corridor leading down into the pyramid, "lest some wild Arabs should be skulkting within to have done us a mischief." But there were no "wild Arabs skulkting."

Then on a hot July day in the summer of 1798 gunpowder on a grand scale was brought to the pyramids of Giza, by Napoleon Bonaparte.

Just three weeks earlier, on June 29, Napoleon had sailed into Alexandria and landed forty thousand well-armed men to conquer Egypt. Bonaparte wanted Egypt as a gateway to India and the East. He had taken Alexandria and his troops were marching toward Cairo when Bonaparte learned that a native army of seventy thousand or more men—thousands of them fierce-fighting Mamelukes mounted on horseback—were massed at Giza in the very shadows of the pyramids, ready to attack.

Reaching the pyramids, where the enemy waited, Bonaparte formed his troops into squares, each square ten men deep, with cannoneers in the center. He ordered his men to hold their fire until the enemy was

An old print illustrating Napoleon's battle with the Mamelukes. Napoleon, on the white horse, gestures toward the pyramids in the background. He is reported to have cried to his troops: "Soldiers, you are about to fight the rulers of Egypt; reflect that from yonder monument forty centuries look down upon you!"

almost upon them. For the army of foot soldiers, greatly outnumbered, this took discipline and courage.

The Mamelukes advanced on their powerful horses with murderous speed. They were fearless, and expert with their great, curved, sharp-edged scimitars. But they were no match for the sudden explosions of gunpowder, the steady barrage of cannons and guns. Within a few hours the "Battle of the Pyramids" was over. The French loss was very slight. It was a complete slaughter of the enemy. And Bonaparte was in control of Egypt.

Napoleon had brought soldiers to conquer the country. But he had also brought with him 150 scholars, known as *savants*, who, in groups, were to study the wonders of Ancient Egypt. Among these wonders, of course, was Cheops's Great Pyramid. The French army had wreathed the Great Pyramid in clouds of gun smoke and the roar of battle. But it was a group of the savants, not soldiers, who unleashed the roar of gunpowder deep inside the Great Pyramid.

The savants probably carried firearms for the same reason the explorers before them had: as protection against unknown dangers. As it turned out, they found no dangers, only excruciating discomfort. These men were not intrepid explorers. Crawling through the cramped, sloping passages was agonizing. The heat and smoke from their torches made the atmosphere almost unbearable. And worst of all were those hordes of bats!

When they finally reached the great inclined gallery of white polished limestone, its shining walls climbing up to a towering ceiling, they felt, as the caliph Mamun and his men had felt almost a thousand years earlier, that they were in a different world. The

Grand Gallery, it was called, and it was well named.

Unlike the caliph's men, the savants had no thought of treasure. They were aware only of the blessed joy of being able to stand, to raise their heads and their eyes, to move freely in spacious magnificence. It brought heady relief, a kind of wild exuberance.

From the height of the Grand Gallery's upper end the savants fired their guns in aimless abandon. They listened first to the great roar, then to the reverberations. Echo after echo after echo finally ended in the sound of distant thunder. They knew of course that to get out of the pyramid they would have to return to the crawl-space passageways, the foul air, and bats. But at the moment there was still time to stand in the spacious splendor and listen to the astonishing series of echoes called forth by the firing of their guns.

However, they had found the interior of the Great Pyramid unpleasant. Afterward they concentrated on examining and surveying the pyramid's exterior. Meantime, at Napoleon's bidding, other groups of savants were studying other wonders and antiquities in Egypt. Later, after Bonaparte abandoned his idea of making Egypt a French protectorate and returned to France, the savants too went home, where they pooled their information and compiled a twenty-four-volume work, *Description de l'Egypte,* which is still of interest today.

While the firing of the guns within the Great Pyramid had been irresponsible and senseless, fortunately no great structural damage had been done.

In the nineteenth century, Richard Howard Vyse, an Englishman, blasted the inside of the Great Pyramid with charges of gunpowder set off in a series of planned and purposeful explosions.

Vyse, a wealthy gentleman, was a colonel in the British army. He was traveling in Egypt for pleasure when he fell under the spell of the Great Pyramid. While interested in its passages and chambers, he believed that in a structure so enormous there were other rooms yet to be discovered. He was an obstinate man, an egoist, and firmly convinced that while other men had searched for the hidden rooms and failed, he, Howard Vyse, would succeed in finding them.

He set up comfortable headquarters in a large empty tomb near the Great Pyramid. Hiring a crew of workmen, Vyse began his explorations.

From the start he had been most intrigued by a discovery a young Englishman had made seventy years earlier. The young man, Nathaniel Davison, was visiting Egypt on his vacation and began exploring the interior of the Great Pyramid purely out of curiosity. In the Grand Gallery Davison noted that when he shouted there was a faint echo. This led him to believe there was an opening of some kind high up in the ceiling. Joining two long poles together with a lighted candle at the tip, he spied a small opening at the top of the Grand Gallery where the ceiling joined the wall. With the help of several Arab workmen, he fastened seven ladders together, leaned the contraption against the smooth limestone wall, and with his helpers steadying the lowest ladder, Davison climbed precariously to the top.

After clearing away an accumulation of bat dung that clogged the opening, Davison wriggled into a narrow passageway through which he crawled for twenty-five feet before reaching a compartment so low it was little more than a crawl space. But Davison found it was the exact length and width of the King's Chamber—its floor, in fact, was the ceiling of the chamber, which lay directly below. The compartment was empty and Davison saw no sign of any opening into other chambers, nothing of interest. So after scratching his name and the date on the wall, he went back out the way he came.

His curiosity about the echo satisfied, Davison went on to explore other parts of the Great Pyramid before his holiday ended and he had to return to England. Back home he wrote about his explorations in the Great Pyramid so that men visiting after him, including Vyse, knew about the crawl space compartment, which they called "Davison's Chamber."

But of all of those who knew about it, Vyse was the only one who thought there might be something beside the solid core of the pyramid beyond it. With some of his work crew to help him, he made a minute examination of the compartment. He found a thin crack in the ceiling in which he could insert a reed. He ordered his men to smash through at that spot with their hammers and chisels. But they found the stone so hard, their efforts were useless. He then brought experienced stonecutters from the quarries across the Nile. But they too were unsuccessful.

Vyse was not a man to admit defeat. He knew another force and how to use it: gunpowder.

With apparently little concern for the splendid red-granite walls and ceiling of the King's Chamber just below, he engaged an Arab who was willing to risk setting off the blasts. It was a dangerous undertaking in the confined space.

When the roar of the explosion, the shower of broken stone and dust, had subsided, Vyse came into the shattered area to examine it. He found that there was indeed another compartment above.

The men crawled into it, and they found the air dense with a strange black powder, which darkened their skin. On examination it proved to be the remains of thousands and thousands of insects imprisoned in ancient times and long since reduced to dust. The force of the explosion had blown the dust into the air.

The first explosion was only the beginning. Having found one compartment, Vyse blasted upward in search of others. For more than three months the explosions roared and echoed through the pyramid, destroying and damaging the ancient masonry. Before he finished, a passage forty feet high had been blasted.

Four compartments had been opened up, one above the other.

These weren't chambers, to be used as rooms. They were empty spaces, cleverly designed by Cheops's builders to protect the flat ceiling of the King's Chamber from the enormous weight of the pyramid that towered above. They are known, accurately, as "relieving compartments." The compartments were never meant to be seen. The stones were rough and undressed and many still bore red ochre identification marks daubed on at the quarry.

Indeed, one of the marked stones proved more interesting than the compartments. On it was written the pharaoh's name—the only instance of Cheops's name found in the pyramid he built. Even so, many archeol-

The Great Sphinx guards the approach to Chephren's Pyramid, second in the Giza complex. It was carved from an outcrop of limestone left by the builders of the Great Pyramid. A recumbent lion 240 feet long and 66 feet high, it has a human head that resembles Chephren's and that wears the royal headdress of the Pharaoh. From time to time the shifting sands that threaten to engulf the Sphinx must be removed. The tale of its first rescue from the desert is recorded on a slab of red granite the Sphinx holds in its outstretched paws. A young prince who stopped to rest near the Sphinx fell asleep and dreamed that the Sphinx spoke, promising him the Double Crown of Egypt if he would clear away the sand. The prince did so, and later, as the great Pharaoh Tuthmosis IV, he did indeed wear the Double Crown, as ruler of both Lower and Upper Egypt.

ogists feel this find was small reward for the damage Vyse's blasting had done.

The colonel took his pyramid explorations seriously and he made some interesting discoveries through the years. But when he wanted to prove a point or reach a goal he was ruthlessly destructive.

As bad as his destruction in the Great Pyramid was, his later attack on the interior of the Third Pyramid at Giza, the pyramid of Mycerinus, was even more devastating. Again certain that there must still be hidden passages and chambers in a structure so large, he let off series after series of blasts, tearing great holes in the pyramid's interior. Nothing was found. And it was Howard Vyse who bored a hole into the Sphinx to see if it was solid. It was.

7
The Mystery of The Well

It had been Nathaniel Davison's discovery of the compartment above the King's Chamber that set Howard Vyse off on his gunpowder assaults. But Young Davison had actually come to the Grand Gallery to examine a hole at the lower end. The hole was cut in the west wall at floor level where the bottom of the Grand Gallery and the upper end of the Ascending Passageway meet. Rough-hewn, about a yard wide, it became known as The Well.

This was the same hole that John Greaves had lowered himself into more than a hundred years before Davison's visit. Bats and foul air sent him back up. After Greaves, all explorers of the pyramid had been baffled by it. Its very location was strange. Why should a crudely cut hole lead down from this splendid, polished limestone gallery? Why had it been cut, and where did it go?

Young Davison was determined to find the answers to these questions before his holiday ended and he had to return to England.

Unlike Greaves, he planned to have some help in making the descent by hiring Arab workmen to lower him on a rope. But hiring help proved difficult. The native Arabs knew The Well and insisted terrible things had happened there. They told of a pasha who had forced some condemned prisoners to crawl down it. Most of the men disappeared forever. The few who survived were said to have come out thirty miles away in the desert, emaciated and incoherent.

The Arabs had another legend about some men who thought there might be treasure in The Well. They lowered one of their fellows into the hole on a rope. The rope broke, and for three hours they could hear his screams echoing fainter and fainter. Leaving the pyramid, they went outside to discuss the horror. Suddenly the lost man appeared, saying, "He who meddles with and covets what does not belong to him is unjust!" And he fell over dead.

However, Davison managed to hire three Arabs to help him. He assured them that all they would have to do was stay at the top and hold a rope with which he would lower himself. The Arabs warned him: he would never return. There were ghosts, evil spirits in The

An old—and inaccurate—drawing of the pyramids and Sphinx at Giza by a European visitor.

Well. One man they knew went down and was seized by a devil.

Nevertheless, tying a rope around his waist, Davison first let down a cord with a lighted candle in a holder. Then, carrying a spare candle, a measure, and a compass (for he didn't know where he might come out), he backed into the hole. He steadied himself on the rough sides as best he could. He had descended about twenty-two feet when he reached a ledge. Below him yawned another hole. He lowered the candle down to see if it would stay lighted in the foul air, and to give him some idea of the depth of the hole. But the shaft was so twisty, its sides so rough, the candle was lost from sight. He pulled it up, relieved to find it still lighted, and decided to go on.

First he had to get one of the Arabs down to the ledge to hold the rope. Using entreaties, threats, and promises of possible treasure, he lured the bravest of the three down. When the workman got to the ledge he was shaking so from fright that Davison wondered if he could trust him to hold the rope. But again he climbed into the hole. Bats swooping around made the descent more difficult.

Snatching occasional toeholds on the rough sides of the shaft, he reached a small, narrow grotto, and thought surely he had hit the bottom. Beside him stood a large stone. Edging his way around it, he stared down into another dark opening, leading into a continuation of the hole.

Throwing a small stone down the hole, he discovered that this third shaft was far deeper than the other two. Trusting that the Arab would remain on the ledge and the rope would hold out, he lowered himself over the edge. He went down, down, wondering if the descent would ever end. Suddenly the shaft began to incline a little off the perpendicular. And soon afterward he reached bottom.

He was in a small pit, filled with sand and rubble and bat dung—and bats. He was sure there must be an exit from the pit, some opening to somewhere. Why else would such a long, difficult passageway through solid stone have been cut? But he could find no opening, no indication of any exit that might have been closed and sealed. He rested briefly, then thought about the danger he was in.

First, there were the bats. He didn't think they would attack him, but he was afraid they might put out his candle and he had no way of relighting it. Then there was the stone beside the hole at the top of the long shaft he had just descended. Possibly he had disturbed the stone. If so, it might shift, closing the opening and sealing him in forever. He started the tortuous ascent.

It was more difficult going up than coming down. When he finally reached the frightened Arab on the ledge at the foot of the first shaft, the candle did go out, plunging them into darkness. The poor Arab was so terrified that Davison instructed him to take hold of the rope and scramble up first. He would follow.

Davison's measurements revealed he had descended a total of 155 feet from the top of the first shaft to the pit at the bottom of the third.

Davison's holiday ended. There was no time for further exploration. He went back to England dissatisfied, still puzzled by The Well. He felt sure that it must lead somewhere. Might there have been an opening

An imaginative drawing of the interior of the Great Pyramid from the 1800s.

from the pit, perhaps sealed, and now hidden by the accumulation of rubble and bat dung?

Some years later, early in the nineteenth century, an Italian ship's captain, G. B. Caviglia, found the answer.

The captain was a strange, solitary man, something of a mystic. From the time he had first heard of

100

the pyramids he was captivated by their aura of wonder and mystery. So when his ship put in at an Egyptian port and he found he had some free time before sailing, he decided to go to Giza.

The sight of the Great Pyramid and the stories he had heard of its interior rooms and passages excited him deeply. He had visions of passages still unexplored, discoveries yet to be made. He let his ship sail without him and prepared to stay in Giza. Though he had little money, he required little—only enough to meet his simple needs and pay a few Arab workmen when help was necessary.

Almost at once Caviglia became interested in The Well. He learned of Davison's descent and his finding nothing at the bottom but a closed, empty pit. Caviglia did not believe that a shaft more than 150 feet deep would have been cut through solid rock to a dead end. Surely Davison had missed something in the pit. He would have to find out.

Much as Davison had done, he made his descent into The Well, all the way down to the pit. There he too found nothing but sand, rubble, and bat dung. Convinced there had to be an exit, he decided to remove the dung and rubble and search. It was soon clear that he needed help. For one thing, there was no place to pile the rubble. It would have to be removed.

He climbed back up and somehow enticed a couple of workmen to go down with him and help him load the rubble into baskets and hoist them up and out.

Very shortly this plan proved impossible. Caviglia had taken down some chunks of sulfur to burn, hoping that would help clear the air, but it was so bad candles wouldn't stay lighted. Working in the pit filled with dust and filth, the men were soon gasping for breath. One workman temporarily lost consciousness. The Arabs refused to stay.

Caviglia burned more sulfur and stubbornly tried to work alone. But he had to give up. To solve the mystery of The Well from the pit, he decided, was impossible.

Caviglia was disappointed. But he knew there were other mysteries in the Great Pyramid to clear up. There was, for example, a room at the bottom of the deep passage known as the Descending Passage. No one had seen it since the Caliph Mamun and his men entered it almost a thousand years earlier. The caliph's men had unwittingly blocked passage to it. They had chopped away the limestone wall to bypass the three granite plugs, and then destroyed the series of limestone plugs that barred their way to the King's Chamber. In doing this, tons and tons of stone had been chipped away, all of which slid down the Descending Passage and piled up from the bottom.

Though no one had been able to reach the room since the caliph's time, its existence was well known. The Greek scholar Strabo had reported it. Other scholars, visiting Giza long before the caliph, had written accounts of crawling down the Descending Corridor to

President Ulysses S. Grant and entourage visit the Great Pyramid in the early 1870s.

the large unfinished chamber. And of course the caliph's description of the room, the first chamber he and his men had entered, was included in accounts of his explorations written by Arab historians.

Caviglia decided to try to clear the passage leading down to the chamber, and again persuaded some Arab workmen to help. The steeply sloping passage was narrow and low ceilinged and packed with rubble. He worked on his hands and knees in the small rough space, loading the rubble into baskets, which the workmen carried out.

He had cleared down a little more than a hundred feet when the fetid air, dust, and heat became so bad he began to cough up blood. He feared he would soon have to stop. But he persevered, and suddenly he smelled sulfur. He was puzzled. Could the smell be coming from the bottom of The Well, where he had burned sulfur not long before?

In the flickering candlelight, through the dust, he saw what appeared to be a low, sealed entryway on the passage wall, and beneath it a hole. Digging in this area, Caviglia and his Arab workmen were hit with a small avalanche of dust and stone—and then a rush of air! In the rubbish that fell on them were the rope and basket he had left in the pit at the bottom of The Well. So it did have an exit—and he had opened it!

Caviglia now knew that The Well linked up with the Descending Corridor. But he still didn't know why.

8

The Tomb Robbers

After Caviglia broke through the Descending Corridor into the bottom of The Well, archeologists were able to solve its mystery. They found out why The Well had been built and who built it.

But before it was solved, other questions had to be answered. First, what was the purpose of the large unfinished chamber that lay deep beneath the pyramid? Excavating the chamber itself and cutting the deep passageway leading to it had been prodigious undertakings. The passage led directly from the pyramid's entrance down more than 350 feet. It went first down through the core of the pyramid, then deep through rock beneath. Its sole purpose had been to connect the entrance with the chamber far below.

Studying the pyramid's interior, the archeologists concluded that the chamber was originally intended to be Cheops's burial chamber. But for some reason they could not determine, plans were changed. The chamber beneath the pyramid was abandoned before it was finished. A new chamber was built far up inside the pyramid itself.

To build a burial chamber up inside the pyramid, a new corridor leading to it had to be made. So at the upper end of the Descending Corridor, almost sixty feet down from the pyramid's entrance, a hole was cut in the Descending Corridor's ceiling. From this opening a new passageway sloping upward into the pyramid was hewn out.

The Ascending Corridor, as it was called, was only about three feet wide and less than four feet high, so men negotiating it had to stoop or crawl. But mercifully it was only 129 feet long. This passageway led to the Grand Gallery, which in turn led to the King's Chamber where the pharaoh would be entombed.

Elaborate plans were devised to make it impossible for anyone to enter the King's Chamber and the passageways leading to it after his burial. Tomb robbers must not get in! Not only would they take the treasures buried with the pharaoh, they would destroy the mummy for the wealth of gold and precious stones within its wrappings.

So, as soon as the king's gold-encased mummy was placed in its granite sarcophagus and the priests

Cheops's empty sarcophagus in the sepulchre chamber of the Great Pyramid. It has been extensively damaged by vandals who hammered it to get pieces of stone as souvenirs.

departed, workmen began blocking off access to the King's Chamber.

First they covered the hole in the Descending Corridor's ceiling with matching stone, cut to fit exactly. Closest scrutiny by the sharpest eyes could not detect that an opening had been there.

With the hole closed, they had sealed off the Ascending Corridor and the way to the burial chamber. But suppose the ceiling block *was* discovered and removed? The Ascending Corridor also had to be blocked so no one could pass through it.

Three large granite plugs and a series of limestone plugs were prepared and stored in the pyramid for this purpose. They rested in the dark recesses on both sides of the Grand Gallery. Even the priests, chanting as they followed the pharaoh's mummy up to the tomb, were not aware of them.

After the burial, the workmen slid them down, one by one, into the Ascending Corridor. When the first plug was packed solid into the lower end of the corridor, the workmen had sealed themselves off from the passageway that led to the pyramid's entrance.

When all the plugs were in place, filling the corridor, a final precaution was taken. In the antechamber three portcullises, large, rectangular stone slabs, were lowered by rope into grooved frames, as an added barrier to the King's Chamber. Surely now the mummy was safe forever.

But now the workmen were sealed in the pyramid with the mummy. How did they get out?

For a long time it was assumed they had been left there to die, their lives sacrificed for the safety of the king's mummy. But modern archeologists who studied

The entrance to the Great Pyramid.

the ancient Egyptians questioned this. They found no
evidence that innocent people were buried alive in ancient Egypt. And they doubted that the workmen
would accept such a fate. Besides, no skeletons, no remains had been found.

No! The workmen had planned their own escape route. It is altogether possible that the pharaoh, and even the men who designed and built the interior passages of the pyramid, did not know about it.

There was a small gap at the upper end of the Ascending Corridor where it joined the Grand Gallery. Here the workmen dug the deep shaft—later known as The Well—that terminated in a small pit they cleverly located near the Descending Corridor. A stone slab was laid to bridge the gap at the top of the shaft and conceal the opening until they needed it.

After the last plug was wedged into place and the stone portcullises were lowered, the workmen climbed down the shaft. At the bottom they cut an opening from the pit into the Descending Corridor.

When the last man went through the opening, it was blocked and sealed, they thought forever. The workmen then climbed up the Descending Corridor and made their way out through the pyramid's regular entrance, which was then sealed also.

The opening from the pit was, of course, the exit Nathaniel Davison had searched for in vain in 1765 and which Captain Caviglia, early in the nineteenth century, crashed through when he was clearing the end of the Descending Corridor.

But Caviglia was not the first man to open it after the escaping workmen had sealed it. Thousands of years before him tomb robbers most certainly had found it. Perhaps one of the workmen had been bribed

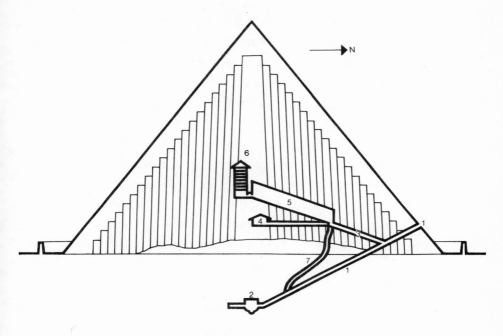

Fig. 10. Interior of the Great Pyramid. From the entrance, a descending corridor (1) leads down into the rock beneath the pyramid to a chamber (2) probably originally intended as the burial chamber. Plans changed and it was decided to put the burial chamber up inside the pyramid. To do so, a hole was cut into the ceiling of the descending corridor, and the ascending corridor (3) was hewn up through the core of the pyramid for 129 feet. Then it opened into a passageway leading to a room (4) probably designed as the burial chamber, now known as the Queen's Chamber. But again plans changed. Continuing upwards from the ascending corridor the magnificent Grand Gallery (5) was built. This led to the King's Chamber (6) where Cheops's sarcophagus was found. At some time a stone was removed from the lower end of the Grand Gallery to reveal a shaft (7) known as The Well, which penetrates the rock beneath the pyramid and links up with the descending corridor near its lower end.

or tortured to tell how he had gotten out of the pyramid. Or perhaps some of the workmen, knowing how to return to the treasure-filled burial chamber, found the temptation too great and robbed it themselves.

Everything in the pyramid was stolen. Even the pharaoh's mummy.

And yet when Caliph Mamun and his men battered an entrance into the pyramid, the stone that concealed the opening in the ceiling was still in place, until their battering rams dislodged it. And crawling through the ceiling opening, the men found the great granite plugs still wedged where the workmen had placed them. They made a formidable block, impossible to pass, until the caliph's men hacked away the limestone walls behind them.

Suppose the escape route had not been devised and the workmen left to perish. Would Cheops's mummy and his treasure have been saved?

Probably not. Somehow the ancient tomb robbers would have gotten in. They always did. No pharaoh buried in a pyramid has ever been found. Every pyramid tomb was plundered, the king's mummy robbed and destroyed.

The devices built in the pyramids to hide and protect the burial chambers were cunning and formidable. There were intricate, twisting passageways with sharp turns, dangerous sudden drops, steep inclines that came to dead ends to baffle intruders. In some pyramids narrow, deep wells were built and filled with

The niche in the Queen's Chamber of the Great Pyramid, probably designed to hold a statue of the Pharoah, was damaged and cut away by vandals seeking treasure.

broken stone. When cleared out, there was nothing but an empty hole. There were trap doors blocked with stones of incredible size. When removed at great effort there was nothing behind them but the solid masonry

The Valley of the Kings.

of the pyramid's core. Some burial chambers had massive walls, with no doors: the mummy was lowered down through an aperture in the ceiling, which was closed with a concealed roof block weighing forty tons or more.

When the Pyramid Age ended, many of these same devices were used to protect the pharaohs' tombs in the Valley of the Kings. These tombs, cut deep in the great rock cliffs, were thought to be impregnable. But they weren't. Robbers got in. They emptied the tombs and stripped the mummies to rob them.

Fortunately, some of these royal mummies were not destroyed. They were rescued, probably by tomb priests, who restored the torn bandages as best they could and reburied the remains. Discovered by archeologists in the late nineteenth century, thirty of these royal mummies can be seen today. Damaged by the ancient tomb robbers, partly unwrapped, they are now safe in the Egyptian Museum in Cairo.

For the robbers the way to the burial chamber was not easy. It was fraught with danger and almost insurmountable obstacles. Sometimes the robbers had help from corrupt tomb priests or guards, or unscrupulous officials who would show them the way for a share of the loot. Even so, the robbers had to be not only wicked but clever and fearless. To be caught would mean torture and certain death. Moreover, anyone who desecrated the mummy faced the wrath of the gods, for a mummy was sacred.

They knew, however, that beneath the lid of the sarcophagus lay wealth beyond belief. Every tomb was a treasure trove. No one knows—it is difficult even to imagine—the wealth of magnificent objects the tombs of the great pharaohs may have held.

But we have an inkling. We know what was found in the tomb of Tutankhamun, the only pharaoh ever found intact.

Tutankhamun's reign was short and unimportant.

He died when he was eighteen. His tomb was in the Valley of the Kings—but it was not cut into the barren cliffs, as the elaborate tombs of more important pharaohs were. Tutankhamun's tomb was dug out of the rock near the valley floor. It was modest: three white-washed rooms and a burial chamber so small there was barely space for his shrine-enclosed sarcophagus.

It was not deeply buried. The English archeologist Howard Carter who discovered it in November 1922 took only three days to shovel away sand and rubble and find a step cut into the rock. It was the first of sixteen steps leading directly down to the tomb.

Yet this modest tomb of an obscure king was filled with dazzling treasures, more than five thousand objects. Seeing them today in the Cairo Museum, one is awestruck by their beauty and opulence. When a sampling of just fifty-eight objects toured the United States in the late 1970s, thousands of people eagerly waited in line for hours for a chance to see them.

After opening the tomb, Carter cut a small opening in the burial chamber door and shone a flashlight through. He saw an expanse of gold. It was the first of four gilt shrines, one inside the other, that almost filled the burial chamber. Inside the fourth was the granite sarcophagus.

When the sarcophagus was opened, Carter found three coffins, nested tightly, each shaped in the form of the young king's mummy. The first and second were of wood covered with gold, inlaid with carnelian and lapis

King Tutankhamun's golden mask photographed in the tomb as it was found by Howard Carter.

lazuli. The third coffin was solid gold—2,448 pounds of twenty-two-carat gold, massive but delicate and elegant, aglow with gems set in graceful designs.

The mummy of the king lay within the gold coffin. Covering the pharaoh's head and extending down to the middle of his body was a mask, wrought of gold, inlaid with gems. It was a likeness of the young king: the eyes luminous, wide open, the shining golden face noble and serene.

Within the wrappings that enfolded him were more than four hundred treasures of rare beauty. On his head was the royal diadem of gold set with turquoise and lapis luzuli. There were golden girdles and pendants, amulets, jewel-studded rings. Gold bracelets encircled his arms.

The small whitewashed rooms outside the burial chamber were crammed with hundreds and hundreds of articles of exquisite workmanship. There were his gold-and-silver throne set with semiprecious stones, an alabaster canopic chest within which lay four small gold and cloisonné coffins containing the embalmed organs from his body. Magnificent chests were filled with royal robes that shone with gold rosettes and sequins, and sandals worked with gold. There were games, silver trumpets, alabaster lamps and vessels, model boats—everything the boy king would want for life in the Afterworld. His ceremonial chariots sheathed with gold were there—dismantled, because they were too large to be drawn through the narrow corridor into the tomb.

It took Carter and his staff six years to empty carefully the rooms of their treasures, record what was there, and move them to safety in the Cairo Museum. Imagine, then, the glories that must have been entombed with the greater kings!

A statue of Anubis guards the entrance of the Treasury in Tutankh-amun's tomb. This photo was taken before anything was removed from the room by Carter's expedition.

The pharaohs ruled Egypt for a thousand years before Tutankhamun and more than a thousand years after. If only one-hundredth part of the treasures buried with the pharaohs had been saved it would be an immense, dazzling treasure trove for the world to cherish.

But those who stole, destroyed. The objects of gold were melted down. The precious stones were pried from their settings to be sold. Gold sheathings were stripped from the furnishings and the wood broken, left to rot. Alabaster lamps and vessels, the carved jars, were emptied of their oils and thrown aside. If Tutankhamun's tomb with its treasures had not survived, the world would not know what it had lost.

However, it is believed that some possessions of the ancient pharaohs may still be found. Not within the tombs, but outside them.

Among the possessions a pharaoh would want in the Afterworld would be his boats. Could it be that somewhere near the Great Pyramid a boat of Cheops might lie buried? There was a young Egyptian archeologist in Cairo who believed so. Late in the 1940s he had an opportunity to find out.

9
The Oldest Boat in the World

Today it is quite possible to scale the Great Pyramid's outside wall, even to reach the top. This has been true ever since the Moslem builders in the fourteenth century removed the smooth white limestone cover, exposing the packing stones, which can be climbed.

From that time on, people have been scaling the pyramid, to various heights and for various reasons. So a young couple attracted little attention when on a bright afternoon in the late 1940s they started to climb up.

They settled down on a smooth ledge to talk. Below them small, shadowy figures of people moved in a soundless, faraway world. Theirs was a place of solitude and quiet, the silence broken only once by a plane flying overhead.

Suddenly from above came a strange, thunderous roar. A moment later the boy was dead, the girl badly injured. A large packing stone—one block out of more than two million stones—had somehow become dislodged and toppled down on them.

No one ever knew what caused the block to move. Some blamed the vibrations from the low-flying plane. Whatever the cause, a young man was dead and a falling stone from Cheops's pyramid had killed him.

People were horrified. The Great Pyramid had stood for almost five thousand years, every stone soundly in place. Now if one stone somehow had worked loose, might not others? It was decided to have a specialist who was familiar with pyramid construction examine its entire exterior, stone by stone.

The man selected to do this job was a young archeologist from Cairo, Kamal el Mallakh. He had degrees in engineering and Egyptology, and he had studied architecture. Furthermore, he was intimately acquainted with the whole Giza complex and knew Cheops's Great Pyramid well.

El Mallakh was pleased with the assignment. But his great archeological interest, while related to pyramids, was not the pyramid itself. It was solar boats, buried near the pyramid so that the pharaoh would have means to travel after death.

Boats were as essential to the pharaoh after death as they had been during his reign on earth. His journey to the next world would be by boat. And in the next world he would travel by boat when he accompanied the sun god, Re, on his trips across the sky in the bright light of day and in the darkness below the earth at night.

Of greatest significance were the two boats intended to transport the pharaoh from this world into the hereafter. This was a long journey, made by both day and night. One boat, known as *maniet*, was for day travel. It arced above the earth, following the sun through the twelve gates of day. After the sun set, the boat for night travel—*masketet*—was to be used. It followed an arced path below the earth through the twelve gates of darkness.

The two arcs made a perfect circle, as round as the sun or the full moon.

No one in modern times had ever seen one of these boats. El Mallakh knew that in the past three boat pits had been found near the Great Pyramid, and as many as five pits near other pyramids. But all were empty.

Would the great Pharaoh Cheops have been satisfied with only three boats for his travels in eternity? He had built the largest pyramid as his tomb and monument. As many as five empty pits had been found near smaller pyramids. Might there not be a large fourth pit hidden somewhere? Possibly a fifth?

As he climbed around the face of the pyramid, el Mallakh often looked down and studied the surrounding area. He knew every inch of it well. He knew where the three empty pits had been located and he began to ponder.

El Mallakh started making mental projections, logically considering where an undiscovered pit might be hidden.

Just south of the Great Pyramid was an empty expanse of sand cluttered with rubble. More and more, el Mallakh's calculations convinced him that a fourth pit would be found there, if there was one.

The rubble was of no interest. He knew what it was. A German archeologist named Junkers had done some excavation on large mastabas just south of the area and thrown the rubble there. But beneath the debris, was there anything more than deep desert sand?

First el Mallakh had to get permission from the Department of Antiquities to dig. Then funds had to be granted to finance the project.

On January 31, 1950, work began.

The rubble was carted away, and the workmen's shovels dipped into the sand. El Mallakh watched closely as the men moved the sand, shovelful by shovelful. He was alert for some change in texture, in color; some indication that men had been here before, that the sand had been disturbed in the past. The sign he watched for might be small, easily missed. But when the sign came, it was bold and surprising.

Suddenly the sand gave way to a hard surface. El Mallakh brushed a patch clean and knelt down to examine it. It was a hardened mud slick. It had to have been laid down by men, the mud carried from the Nile. But why would a "floor" of mud be laid here, only forty feet from the Great Pyramid, in the desert?

It was a camouflage, el Mallakh decided, placed there to conceal something. When all the sand was cleared away, the slick was surprisingly long, about 120 feet, and tapered at each end. What was it hiding?

The only sound was the chip-chip-chip of the small picks and mallets chiseling away at the hard slick. A space was cleared, the debris brushed away, and the men saw that beneath the slick was a slab of limestone. Every man in the crew was excited now.

When the entire slick was finally removed, they gazed down in wonder at the great expanse of Tura limestone—forty-two blocks in all, laid with skill and precision, the thin seams between each block sealed with gypsum. Surely the gleaming white limestone would have been brought from Tura and laid there for only one purpose: to serve as a gigantic roof to protect Cheops's boat when it was buried almost five thousand years before.

El Mallakh knew he had found the boat pit.

But he thought of all the other boat pits that had been opened with hope and excitement, and that had always been empty.

Since the boat would have been built of wood, el Mallakh's first fear was its destruction by termites, white ants. He remembered the devastation in the tomb of Queen Heterpheres, Cheops's mother, when it was opened in modern times. Originally filled with beautiful furniture of wood faced with solid gold, nothing remained but the golden sheathings lying helter-skelter on the floor. Every bit of wood had been destroyed by termites. The tomb's thick rock walls, the great stone roof blocks, the deep cover of desert sand, had not protected the wood from the white ant.

Or might tomb robbers have been there?

A full-sized boat, ordered by Cheops for his use in eternity, would be elegantly made and of great value.

El Mallakh studied the limestone roof. There was no sign of damage, and that was reassuring. But the limestone roof was only one entrance to the pit. For the ancient thieves, skilled in tunneling their way into any tomb they wanted to enter, robbing the boat pit would not have been difficult. Was the boat there?

The simplest and safest way to find out was to use an electric drill to bore a small hole into the pit through one of the limestone blocks. But there was no electricity at the site of the pit. El Mallakh looked up at the Great Pyramid. Some electric wiring had been installed there—the King's Chamber, he knew, had lights.

Soon a long wire was run up the side of the pyramid through a small vent into Cheops's burial chamber, and the hand drill bit into the stone.

When the drill stopped, el Mallakh knelt down and put his face close to the small opening.

The fragrance that rose from the pit filled him with joy. It was the scent of cedar, and a sweet aroma

126

of spices and incense. Later el Mallakh said, "There was a fragrance as of a great cathedral."

The boat would have been built of the finest cedar. And placed in a pit with spices, incense, sweet herbs, to preserve it. This was a day and date el Mallakh would always remember: bright noon on May 26, 1954.

He took a mirror from his pocket. Holding it so it caught the sun, he shone it down into the hole. In the pale reflected light of the sun he saw a tip of an oar. His joy was complete.

When the first block of limestone was moved, el Mallakh saw that the ancient Egyptians had provided further protection for the boat by spreading matting beneath the stone blocks. The gypsum sealing the stones together crumbled and fell harmlessly on the matting. Lifting the matting carefully, el Mallakh peered down for his first look at the boat.

But was it a boat?

Inside the pit, closely packed in a most orderly way, he saw pieces of wood in varying shapes and sizes. There were slender poles, an oar, coils of rope, the end of a keel. Cheops's boat had been built, then dismantled before it was placed in the pit.

Why had it been dismantled? The first assumption was that the pit had been dug and found to be too small. So the boat had been taken apart for burial.

El Mallakh did not believe this. The ancient Egyptians were masters at measuring accurately and fitting things together precisely. The pyramid itself had been

127

built to meet exact measurements. People who knew how to build so accurately would not have made such a mistake. Or if by some chance they had, they would have enlarged the pit.

El Mallakh thought the boat had been dismantled for two reasons. One, it would be far less tempting to thieves. A handsomely constructed boat, ready for use on the nearby Nile, would be a valuable piece of property. The same boat, packed away in hundreds of separate pieces, would be of little use or value.

Secondly, the dismantled boat would be less vulnerable to decay from the atmosphere. In compact layers, the boat was stored in a virtually airtight compartment.

Today we might ask how the pharaoh could use a dismantled boat for his travels in eternity. To ancient

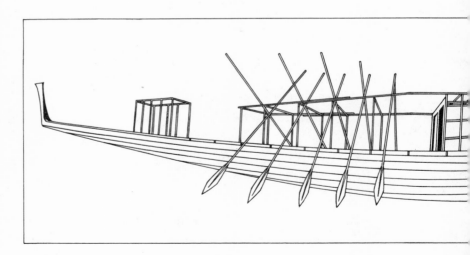

Egyptians the answer was simple: the spirits knew how to put the boat back together in a moment of magic. It would be ready for use as soon as the king needed it.

To el Mallakh, however, the dismantled boat posed some special problems. Before a single piece could be moved, a shed to protect the pieces and provide a place for the boat's reconstruction had to be built.

As soon as the shelter-workshop was ready, the tedious job of removing the pieces from the pit began. It took el Mallakh and his men eighteen months to empty the pit. Every part was handled with time-consuming care. Each piece was examined, measured precisely, photographed, catalogued, and recorded in detail.

In all there were 1,224 pieces, each piece num-

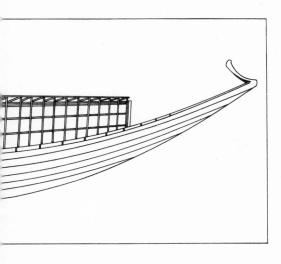

Fig. 11. Cheops's 143 foot boat, which he had built to transport himself after death from the earth to his home in the next world.

bered and fitted into thirteen layers in the pit. Packed among the pieces were coils of rope, almost fifteen thousand feet, woven of fine linen and plant fibers. The ancient Egyptians had packed the dismantled boat with such skill and care that every bit of wood and the lengths of rope had survived more than 4,750 years of burial in excellent condition.

The boat was built of the finest wood obtainable—cedar of Lebanon, which grew on the mountain slopes of distant Phoenicia. Only the choicest trees would have been selected, and they had to be of a great size, since even the largest parts of the boat were carved from a single piece of wood.

Studying the wood today, archeologists estimated that the trees had been of great age when cut—probably five thousand years old. The wood dated back ten thousand years.

El Mallakh held a piece in his hand and marveled that after all that time nothing in the wood had been lost or changed. The cedar still retained its rich brown luster, its fragrance. But even more impressive was the perfection with which each piece had been crafted by those ancient workmen with their primitive tools. From the slenderest small pole to the large, gracefully curved keel, each part was superbly fashioned and finished. Many pieces could stand on their own as works of art. Cheops had summoned the realm's finest craftsmen to build his boat.

The day el Mallakh looked down into the pit for

the first time and saw the boat dismantled, he realized it was going to be an almost impossible task to reassemble it. No one in the world knew what the boat had looked like originally. There were no pictures, no diagrams. No boat like it had ever been found before. There were no models, nothing with which to compare it.

El Mallakh had discovered the boat. But he could not put it back together. If the job were bungled, he would blame himself always for having opened the pit. Restored, it had to be the same boat Cheops had ordered to be built. The same boat the pharaoh had accepted with royal approval.

There was only one man el Mallakh knew he could trust with the job. His name was Ahmed Youssef Moustafa. He was one of the greatest restorers of antiquities in Egypt, perhaps in the world. Studying the fragments of an ancient treasure, Moustafa had a kind of genius for knowing how to put them together again, recreating the object in its original beauty.

El Mallakh had to have Moustafa. But getting him would not be easy. He knew where Moustafa was. He was 185 miles up the Nile at ancient Thebes, working on a tomb restoration in the Valley of the Kings. El Mallakh also knew that the officials and the archeologists responsible for the Theban project would not willingly let Moustafa go.

In order to bring him to Giza, el Mallakh would have to convince certain people that no restoration job in all Egypt was at that time as important as the reconstruction of Cheops's boat, and that only Moustafa could do it.

It took el Mallakh more than two years to bring Moustafa to Giza—more than two years of arguing, negotiating, persuading, and cutting red tape. During that time the shed had been built, the pit emptied, and some preliminary work done on reassembling the boat.

But not until the day Moustafa walked into the reconstruction shed to go to work did Kamal feel that restoration of the boat had truly begun. It was to take fifteen years to complete the job. Even Moustafa's genius could not hurry it.

Each step began as a theory, to be worked out, planned, tested on paper. It was a complex puzzle of more than a thousand pieces. A few pieces were easily identified: the keel, and the twelve oars, each twenty-seven feet long and identical in their strong, graceful design. But there were hundreds of other unrecognizable pieces in different shapes and sizes. And there were more than five hundred poles and rods, varying in length and thickness, that must fit somewhere. But where?

Many of the wooden parts had U-shaped holes carved in them. Each U was perfectly formed, a marvel of carpentry for men working with simple hand tools. Soon the reason for the U-shaped holes was recognized. At the same time it became understandable why so much rope was found with the dismantled boat. The whole boat—keel, deck, superstructure—had been lashed together with rope threaded through the U-shaped holes. This construction gave the boat stability with flexibility. So important was the use of rope in the boat's construction that the ancient Egyptians had packed much more rope than was needed, just in case some deteriorated.

Examining the parts, it was clear that each piece, even the smallest, was cut precisely to size and carved to fit perfectly where it belonged.

Except for a few small copper joints, no metal had been used. There were no nails, bolts, or screws, not even wooden pegs, to make the job of reassembling easier. The principle of construction relied entirely on the accurately cut pieces fitting tightly together, and the rope threading tautly through the U-shaped holes.

As the reconstruction progressed, the men who worked and the men who watched saw an object of great beauty taking shape. They no longer wondered if the individually beautiful pieces would make a harmonious whole when put together.

El Mallakh watched Moustafa and his staff put on the finishing touches. He had discovered the dismantled boat in its pit on May 26, 1954. Now, on September 15, 1971, it stood complete, 143 feet long and 26 feet high at its tallest point. Its simple lines combined grace and strength and elegance, as befitted a boat built for a great pharaoh's voyage to eternity.

It was the boat Cheops had commissioned. At his death it had probably been in the pharaoh's funeral procession, gliding down the Nile from the capital city of Memphis to the pyramid site at Giza.

Some say it could sail the Nile today. Every part of its structure is as sound and functional as it was in Cheops's day.

But it will be protected in the air-conditioned structure built for it above the pit where it was found. It is the oldest boat known in the world. And the only boat of its kind in the world today.

El Mallakh, seeing it finally finished, said quietly, "The boat was sleeping for almost five thousand years. Now it lives."

Nearby, also in the shadow of the Great Pyramid, is another boat pit. El Mallakh is certain that a boat of the same beauty, a sister ship, lies there "sleeping," waiting to be reassembled. He feels sure it is there because after the white limestone blocks protecting the first boat were uncovered, he detected another stretch

Cheops's solar boat inside the glass structure built especially to house it. In this 1980 photo, members of an Israeli delegation to Egypt view the world's oldest boat.

135

of Tura limestone slabs laid on the same line, but to the west.

Someday that pit, too, will be opened. El Mallakh hopes it will be soon! However, it has been decided not to open it until scientific preparations can be made to handle its contents. This means building a permanent, air-conditioned structure in which the work of reassembling can be done in safety and where the finished boat can be properly exhibited.

To build such a structure is costly. And the pit will remain closed until funds for the undertaking are available.

10
Finding a Buried Pyramid

Buried beneath the sand along the Nile, lost pyramids await discovery. The superstructure, which once rose in pointed glory to the sky, may no longer be there. It may have been stolen, the stones quarried to be used in other structures. Or the pyramid may have been left unfinished, never reaching its capstone peak.

Deeply buried under the sand and rubble, the great wall enclosing the pyramid may be found, and within the enclosure the first tiers of the pyramid, coursing upward. Most important, the pyramid's substructure may be there, cut far down in the rock, with its corridors and shafts and pits. And perhaps a burial chamber with some trace of the pharaoh who built the tomb.

In recent times such a pyramid was found and unearthed by an Egyptian archeologist, M. Zakaria Goneim.

For a long time, and well into the twentieth century, trained archeologists came to Egypt from Europe and the United States. Then a new generation of archeologists appeared. They were young Egyptians, the earlier ones trained by Western professors, mostly at the University of Cairo. Among these was young Goneim, a brilliant and gifted student who, right out of school, was given a post in the Department of Antiquities and stationed in Saqqara.

Goneim loved Saqqara. He spent a great deal of time studying the entire necropolis. The Step Pyramid stirred him most. The earliest of Egypt's pyramids, it was built by the pharaoh Zoser and his architect, Imhotep, in the Third Dynasty, almost five thousand years before Goneim was born.

The department sent him to other parts of Egypt on archeological assignments, and it was several years before he returned to Saqqara as chief inspector and keeper of the Saqqara necropolis.

There in his small white house, a mere dot on the vast desert plateau, Goneim lived within sight of the magnificent Step Pyramid and the whole necropolis.

All the time he had been away, something about Saqqara had puzzled him. Zoser, he knew, was listed as the first king of the Third Dynasty. And Zoser had chosen to build his Step Pyramid tomb at Saqqara because that was the most important necropolis in all

Egypt at that time. It overlooked the capital city of Memphis, where earlier kings had lived and reigned.

But the Third Dynasty had lasted approximately a hundred years. Other kings had followed Zoser. Seeing the awe that Zoser's pyramid inspired, would they not have wanted to build pyramids of their own nearby?

There were none to be seen. Other pyramids were within view, to be sure. But all had been built by pharaohs of later dynasties. Only Zoser's could be credited to the Third.

The necropolis stretched about four and a half miles long, a mile across at its widest, along the desert plateau. Goneim walked back and forth in the sand and heat, as Imhotep had done centuries earlier. He walked past mastaba tombs older than the Step Pyramid, and pyramids built after it, and excavations made by earlier Western explorers, until he knew every inch of the necropolis.

He pinpointed a rectangular area a short distance to the southwest of the Step Pyramid's enclosure wall. Goneim detected fragments of alabaster and worked limestone in the sand and an occasional rubble outcrop. He wanted very much to see what was underneath.

His department provided a small grant, and in September of 1951 Goneim prepared to dig. Luckily he was able to get Hofni Ibrahim to head his work crew. Hofni had worked on digs with several top Western archeologists. He gathered together a small crew of experienced workmen.

Goneim could not afford any mistakes or false starts. The money would run out all too soon. With Hofni's help he minutely examined every inch of the site. They decided to begin at the western edge, where they found a small outcrop of rubble masonry.

But before digging started, Goneim had to face a problem that can be time-consuming to the scrupulous archeologist. He had to find an acceptable place to dump the tons and tons of rock, sand, and rubble to be removed while excavating. Often after a dump site had been selected, fragments of ancient statuary, pot shards, and even remnants of a wall or mastaba were found buried beneath the surface. Not wanting to cover objects of value with tons of debris, the archeologist must then look elsewhere. This might happen several times before a suitable dump site was located. Goneim was lucky—sinking trial pits in the first site he selected, he found only rock strata.

Next Goneim had a light narrow-gauge railway laid down to carry the debris from the digs to the dump. Known as a Decauville railway, it could be rapidly installed and easily moved when necessary. Workmen loaded the small open-top cars, then pushed them to the dump where they tipped the cars to unload them.

With the railway in place, preparations were complete. On a bright, sunny morning, September 27, 1951, work began.

To their amazement, on the first day Goneim and his crew struck what appeared to be an ancient wall of gray limestone. Continuing to excavate, they found that the wall enclosed a large rectangular area. Dull limestone, unpolished, unadorned, it was not prepossessing. Goneim decided it was actually the foundation for a wall. Finding fragments of Tura limestone nearby, he deduced that originally a gleaming white wall had stood on top of the gray foundation.

Though the wall was gone, its Tura limestone undoubtedly taken by later builders, Goneim was heartened by the discovery of the large, rectangular, graystone foundation. Surely the ancient Egyptians would not have built a great enclosure wall unless they had something important to enclose. Perhaps a pyramid! He was sure if they continued digging in the area, something would be discovered.

Week after week the excavating went on, and nothing was found. Then on New Year's Day, 1952—a joyous day, Goneim later said—they uncovered what appeared to be the end of a limestone wall. Gradually as the deep stone rubble was carefully removed the wall began to emerge in all its white magnificence. It was three months before the wall was completely uncovered and stood gleaming in the sun. It had no relation to the wall that once stood on the gray foundation. And it was a mystery. Handsomely constructed, it led nowhere. It ran 138 feet and stopped. Furthermore, it was intact. Clearly it had been purposely buried beneath the sand and rubble shortly after it was built.

Studying the wall, Goneim saw with growing excitement that in design and workmanship it was very similar to Zoser's pyramid wall. Its construction was typical of only that period, the Third Dynasty. Goneim concluded that it had been built not long after Zoser's reign, probably by his successor.

Surely the wall had not stood alone!

During the three months that the White Wall, as the men called it, was being uncovered, Goneim had put Hofni in charge of a small crew to investigate the nearby surrounding area. He hoped for some sign indicating a pyramid—perhaps an opening that might lead to an entrance, or an outcrop of masonry.

One day a workman shouted that he had uncovered a rough-cut hole. Goneim and Hofni saw it was a crude opening obviously made by ancient tomb robbers. Goneim's hopes were raised, but also his fears. Tomb robbers would not have tunneled down through the rock unless they felt sure of reaching a burial chamber. If they reached it, the chamber would have been plundered.

Goneim climbed into the opening. Hofni followed. For sixty-two feet they crawled down a rough tunnel that curved in a wide semicircle. Braving falling stones and the possibility that the tunnel might cave in, they suddenly reached solid rock, where the tomb robbers had given up. They crawled out, relieved that the robbers had gone no farther. Still, they had found no evidence of a pyramid.

142

Then came a discovery that proved to be a breakthrough. Goneim, working not far from where Hofni and his crew were excavating, heard Hofni calling to him excitedly. They had struck masonry! Goneim rushed over to examine it. As more of the masonry was slowly, carefully uncovered, it appeared to be the corner of a large structure.

Goneim's hopes soared. Could it be the corner of a step pyramid? He believed it was. He wanted desperately to go ahead with the excavating and find out.

Unhappily, this was not possible. It was the beginning of May, when the intense heat of summer ended the digging season until fall. Of even greater concern to Goneim, the funds allowed him had been used up. For Goneim, time and money had run out.

For a year and a half work at the site stood still. During that time Goneim studied and evaluated the work that had been done, and he managed to arrange for a grant that would let him go ahead.

On a pleasant November day, with Hofni at his side, he was able to resume. They started work at the outcrop of masonry they had found earlier. The clamor of a dig had never sounded happier to Goneim: the voices of the workmen shouting and singing, the noisy clatter of the little railroad.

As excavation continued, Goneim saw to his joy that the large edifice they were uncovering was of step-pyramid construction. It was a series of independent walls, sharply inclined, leaning one against the other, and the horizontal stone courses, or tiers, were laid at right angles to the slope of the walls. This was exactly the construction Imhotep had devised when he built Zoser's Step Pyramid!

Goneim had uncovered one corner of a step pyramid.

The other three corners and part of the first step were soon exposed. Measuring the base, Goneim found each side was 395 feet long, making its perimeter slightly larger than that of Zoser's pyramid. Using this and other measurements he was able to calculate that the pyramid had been designed to rise seven steps, to a height of about 230 feet. It might never have been completed to its full height, however. It was impossible for Goneim to tell, since all the upper steps had long since disappeared. Probably they had been plundered and appropriated by later pharaohs for their own monuments. When Goneim found the pyramid, the highest point remaining was twenty-three feet.

In any case, it was the area beneath the pyramid that fired Goneim's imagination. For there, cut deep in bedrock, should lie the pharaoh's burial chamber. To reach it would not be easy. First the entrance to the tomb would have to be found. The ancient Egyptians always made this as difficult as possible.

Goneim noticed a depression in the sand about seventy-five feet north of the pyramid. He excavated and found an inclined trench cut in the rock. With Hofni and a small crew he made his way down the trench. Progress was slow. At intervals the men had to remove barriers of stone walls. But it led them to a large doorway cut in the rock and sealed solidly with a door block of masonry.

This had to be the entrance to the tomb!

Fearfully Goneim examined the sealed door block. It was intact! He wanted desperately to open it then and there. But first he had to report his find to the Department of Antiquities and wait for the arrival of government officials.

When the door block was broken open, Goneim and the officials climbed through into a high, steeply descending corridor. After about sixty feet they were stopped by an accumulation of large stones and rubble that filled the corridor from floor to ceiling. There was no way of going on. Disappointed, Goneim led the frustrated officials back up the steep corridor into the sunshine. Later he went back to make a careful examination. Where had the stones come from?

He found a square opening cut in the ceiling of the corridor above the stone pile. It was difficult to see because stones and rubble were piled roof-high. The stones had fallen down through this hole, which was surely the bottom opening of a shaft. But where was the top?

Outside, Goneim and his crew searched the whole area of the pyramid's superstructure for two days before they found it. Beneath a cover of sand and rubble, they found a shaft, its opening blocked with stones.

145

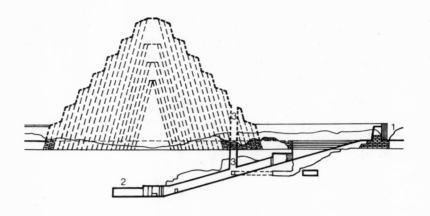

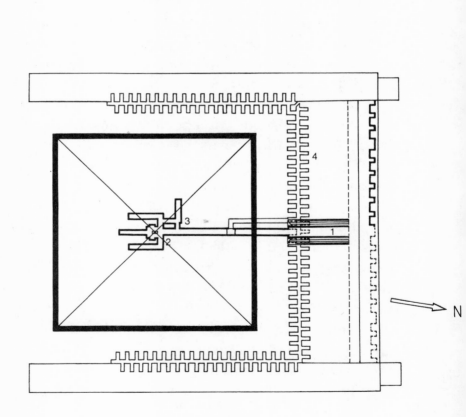

146

Lifting the stones out, the men found the remains of a large number of mummified animals—goats, oxen, gazelles, dogs. They had been carefully buried in layers, some wrapped in linen, each layer separated by a covering of sand. In the bottom layer was a collection of papyri, sixty-two documents written not in ancient hieroglyphs but in a script used much later, about 600 B.C. The documents and the animals had been placed in the shaft two thousand years after the pyramid was built. Probably members of a religious cult had used it as a burial place for religious documents and their sacred animals. Yet it was quite possible that the men who placed them there might have climbed down the shaft and discovered the burial chamber.

Beneath the papyri the shaft was filled with large stones. Goneim was relieved to see that they had not been disturbed since the ancient builders had pushed

Fig. 12. (Top) The Buried Pyramid of Sekhem-Khet, section facing west. (Bottom) Substructure and ground plan of Sekhem-Khet's Pyramid. Excavating about 75 feet north of the pyramid, M. Zakaria Goneim found the entrance to a tunnel (1) descending deep beneath the pyramid and leading to the burial chamber (2). Among the many obstacles blocking the way was a shaft (3) rising up through the subterranean rock and the core of the pyramid, down which the ancient Egyptians had dropped tons of stones, creating a barrier more than 15 feet thick. In the complex substructure were 132 storerooms (4) opening off corridors extending on three sides.

them down into the shaft, stone after stone after stone. The shaft, it seemed clear, had been part of the pyramid's original construction. It had been built so the stones could be dropped down to block the corridor after burial.

Goneim realized he could clear the barrier of stone in the corridor only by working in the shaft from the top down.

The shaft was about half cleared when there was a fatal accident. A workman tumbled down the shaft and was suffocated by falling debris.

Goneim was shocked and saddened by the tragedy, but he was unprepared for what followed. Hundreds of people gathered at the site from nearby villages. Some were angry and threatening. Rumors spread that the pyramid had collapsed and scores of men had been killed. Carloads of curious people came from Cairo and Giza, adding to the chaos and confusion.

All the laborers who worked at the site quit. They refused to come near the pyramid, fearing a curse from the pharaoh who had built it. Not for several weeks did things calm down and work resume.

The ancient Egyptians had thrown a lot of stone down the shaft to protect their pharaoh. The stone barrier filled the corridor for a distance of fifteen feet.

When all the stones were finally cleared away, a thick layer of clay was uncovered. Hidden under the clay Goneim and his men found hundreds of beautiful vessels, bowls and vases carved from alabaster and other fine stones. The ancient Egyptians had protected them with the thick padding of clay. They knew what they were doing—only a few on the top were crushed by the weight of the stone. Beneath them, all were whole and as beautiful as the day they were buried.

Soon after this discovery one of the men noticed a faint glint of gold in the clay near the corridor wall. Gently clearing away the clay, Goneim found a small cache of gold jewelry—twenty-one armlets and bracelets, and most beautiful of all, a golden piece in the shape of a scallop shell, hinged so that the shell opened and closed. Probably it was a container for cosmetics.

The find was unique, and important for two reasons. First, no gold jewelry from the Third Dynasty had ever been found before. Second, finding jewelry in a tomb was almost positive proof that a burial had taken place there.

The next discovery Goneim made in the corridor, while not beautiful to look at, was so important that he later declared it "meant almost as much to me as finding the pyramid itself."

The find was five small, buff-colored jars topped with dry clay stoppers. Goneim's hope was that there might be a seal imprint on the stoppers. So far he did not know who had built the pyramid, or what pharaoh's tomb it was meant to be. Sometimes a seal found in a tomb bore the owner's name.

Handling them with great care—for they were

149

very fragile—he brushed them gently with a soft brush and applied a fixative. In a strong light, with a magnifying glass, he studied each small clay stopper.

Faint, but discernible, he saw the impressions of a royal seal. He saw the hieroglyphic sign of a pharaoh's name. It was Sekhem-Khet, "Powerful of Body."

The king hitherto had been unknown. His name had not appeared on any of the Egyptian king lists. Now it would be added. For more than four thousand years the pharaoh Sekhem-Khet had been lost. Goneim had found him.

Meantime the work of clearing the corridor continued, and hopes of reaching the burial chamber were high. Then suddenly the corridor ended in a great mass of rock.

After examining it, Goneim felt certain that construction had stopped at this point. The project had been abandoned by the ancient builders. This conclusion was greatly strengthened by the fact that the sides of the corridor were rough and unfinished. It was useless to go on, he decided. There would be no burial chamber.

Also, the heat of summer was upon them again. The corridor, beneath more than a hundred feet of sunbaked rock and sand, was stiflingly hot and airless.

But Hofni did not agree. "We are in the heart of the pyramid," he protested. "We should not stop."

The crew was willing to continue. So they began the arduous job of hacking away at the mass, wondering if they would find anything other than solid stone beyond it.

For weeks in stifling heat they excavated through the great mass of rock. Then they hit a block of masonry with the outline of a doorway. Hopes soared again!

A hole was cut in the masonry—it was ten feet thick. Goneim, electric torch in hand, crawled through on his belly. Hofni followed.

Emerging, Goneim found himself near the ceiling of a chamber, with nowhere to go but down. With Hofni literally at his heels, he hit the floor. (Later they found that the chamber was seventeen feet high. Their fall was eased by the fact that the floor was covered with a thick layer of clay.)

Scrambling to their feet, they flashed their lights into the blackness. Suddenly there was a luminous glow of light as the beams, piercing the darkness, struck a magnificent sarcophagus of pale, golden alabaster.

Awed as Goneim was by its splendor, his first thought was: Is it intact? He moved toward it. On the top was a funeral wreath placed there at the time of the burial. The leaves were dried and fragmented. He flashed his light along the top to see if the lid had been disturbed. But there was no lid. The sarcophagus had been carved out of one great block of alabaster.

Kneeling down to examine the sides, he saw that it was a solid block, except that one end was covered by an alabaster panel, designed to slide upward to receive the pharaoh's body, after which the panel was dropped back into place and sealed.

Feverishly he examined the edges of the seal, the traces of plaster at the joints. All was intact!

This was enough to send any archeologist into a frenzy. Only one pharaoh had ever been found undisturbed in his tomb: Tutankhamun. And no pharaoh had ever been found in a pyramid tomb.

Again he ran his light along the edges of the panel. There was no doubt that the sarcophagus, sealed at the time of burial, had never been touched. The pharaoh's body within would be intact.

Goneim and Hofni stared at the beautiful alabaster box in wonder, almost unable to believe the moment was real.

Then one by one, the workmen, anxious to know what had been found, began dropping through the hole down onto the floor. For several minutes there was awed silence. Suddenly with shouts of excitement the men circled in a dance around the golden alabaster sarcophagus. Goneim and Hofni joined them. Men were embracing each other in congratulation, weeping with joy. After years of hard work, a wondrous discovery had been made, and they were part of it. Shortly the emotional frenzy ended and the room grew quiet. They all moved back from the opalescent beauty of the sarcophagus and stood in respectful silence. Then one by one, Goneim, Hofni, all of them scrambled up the wall, helping each other as best they could, and crawled back through the opening.

Four weeks later—four years after the work had started—a small group of officials gathered to witness the opening of the sarcophagus. The door block had been removed and electric lights installed. The alabaster sarcophagus shone brilliantly in the lighted chamber. Goneim knew the panel would be heavy—it proved to weigh about five hundred pounds. Scaffolding had been built and a pulley hung to lift the panel. There were two holes in the top of the panel into which Goneim fitted specially made steel hooks.

The atmosphere in the room was tense. Goneim signaled the two workmen manning the ropes to go ahead. They pulled and pulled. But the panel didn't budge. Two other men joined them, then two more. Finally with six men pulling and striving, sweat pouring from their bodies, the panel slowly moved upward about one inch. Goneim ordered wedges to be placed in the opening and examined the panel to make sure no damage had been done. He saw then that the tightly fitted panel had been solidly sealed with plaster and glue.

After two hours of terrible effort, the panel slowly began to rise. Goneim knelt down and looked inside the sarcophagus.

It was empty.

Everyone in the room stood in stunned silence. Methodically Goneim examined the inside of the sarcophagus. Using a lamp of high wattage, he searched for some clue—marks on the stone made when a coffin was inserted; a spot of discoloration; a fragment or print of some kind. There was nothing. The interior was pristine.

It had not been robbed. No seals were broken. Tomb robbers could never have raised the heavy panel and replaced it without telltale signs. Nor would they have bothered replacing it.

Had the empty sarcophagus been placed there while the king lived, in anticipation of his death? No. If so, it would not have been so solidly, permanently sealed. The funeral wreath would not have been placed on top. Goneim proposed no answer to the mystery.

Others have surmised that the pharaoh's body, with all its valuables, was stolen before burial. Those who placed the sarcophagus in the chamber and laid the funeral wreath on top did not know the sarcophagus was empty.

The empty sarcophagus was a crushing disappointment to Goneim. To make a great and spectacular discovery is every archeologist's dream. But as a scholar Goneim knew that every find, large or small, is important. Even one alabaster pot, one gold bracelet brought to light is significant because it speaks of the past.

In discovering and opening up Sekhem-Khet's pyramid Goneim had illuminated parts of Egypt's ancient past that had been buried in darkness for almost five thousand years. He had restored a lost pharaoh to history. He had brought to light a beautiful sarcophagus, rare because it was found in a step pyramid and dated back to the Old Kingdom.

And he had found a pyramid.

There are other pyramids in Egypt hidden beneath the sand, waiting to be discovered. In one of these there may be a sarcophagus, seals intact, and within it the pharaoh in his coffin, undisturbed since burial.

11
The Pyramids
of the Indians

The only other pyramid builders in the world were the Indians of Central America and Mexico.

The fact that the pyramid structure was developed by two entirely different cultures, oceans apart on opposite sides of the earth, is a baffling coincidence.

Long before the fierce Aztec warriors conquered most of Central Mexico, between A.D. 1300 and 1500, numerous cultures had flourished there—notably the Olmec, Toltec, Teotihuacan, and Zapotec. The Olmecs, Toltecs, and the people of Teotihuacan left pyramids that are well-known today. And the Maya, far to the east in Yucatan and south into present-day Guatemala and Honduras, were the busiest of builders, constructing countless pyramids.

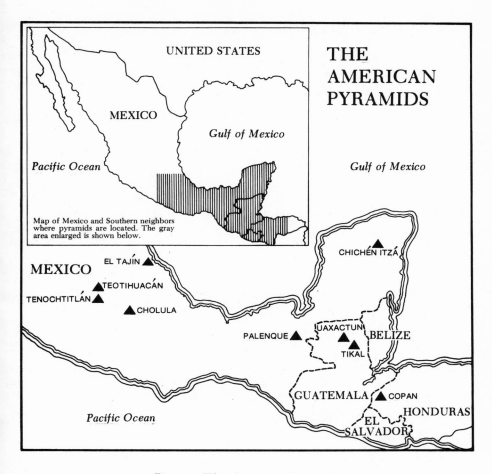

Fig. 13. The American Pyramids.

There is guesswork aplenty but no known reason why the pyramid cult should have existed in two civilizations as different and as far apart as those of Egypt and the American Indians. The pyramids each built were very different. Moreover, there was a lapse of well over a thousand years between the time pyramid building was discontinued in Egypt and begun by the Indians in the Western world.

Not only were the Indian pyramids different from the Egyptian in construction and design, they served a different purpose. The Indian pyramids were not built as tombs, to house the dead. They were built for rituals and worship. Though pyramidal in shape, none rose to a capstone apex. The Indian pyramid had a flat summit upon which a temple stood, dedicated to one of their many gods.

From the base of the pyramid a steep staircase led up to the temple. Here, on the pyramid's summit, the Indians conducted their rites, including human sacrifices.

Since the Indian pyramid was essentially a pedestal for the temple's dramatic setting, it required no interior construction of corridors and chambers as the Egyptian pyramids did. The core, or interior, was a solid mass of tightly packed stones, or sometimes chunks of adobe brick, gravel, and soil. The core was held in place with thick outer walls made of stones mixed with adobe or building stones held together with mortar.

No one knows how many pyramids the ancient Indians erected—probably hundreds and hundreds, counting the many small ones. A number are still standing today.

Pyramid of the Sun, Teotihuacan, Mexico. The people standing on the top give an idea of the pyramid's enormous size.

One of the largest is the Pyramid of the Sun, about thirty miles north of Mexico City. Close by is the slightly smaller Pyramid of the Moon.

The Pyramid of the Sun once dominated the great religious center of Teotihuacan. On its summit, in front of the temple, stood a giant statue of the Sun God, wearing a breastplate of solid gold that reflected rays of golden light. Though the statue and its golden splendor are gone and the temple destroyed, the pyramid, built hundreds of years ago, is magnificent and impressive.

Its base is about the same size as that of Cheops's Great Pyramid at Giza, although it is less than half as high. Modern archeologists questioned whether a structure as large as the Pyramid of the Sun could have been built with an interior made of soil, gravel, and stone alone. They thought in a pyramid of its size the

159

Indians must have used another type of construction, or that the pyramid had been built around another, smaller pyramid, which served as its core.

They bored two tunnels into the pyramid for exploration. They found the Pyramid of the Sun had been built in the usual way. The great mass of soil, gravel, and stone that forms its interior is held in place only by the outer walls, which are fifty to sixty-five feet thick. No inner pyramid was found.

However, building a second pyramid around an existing one was not unusual in Indian pyramids. Such ruins were found of a very large pyramid believed to have exceeded Cheops's Great Pyramid in bulk. Discovered at Cholula, about eighty miles east of Teotihuacan, the first and innermost pyramid was created about the same time as the Pyramid of the Sun.

During the centuries that followed, at least four additional pyramids were built, one upon the other, enlarging the original structure to an enormous size. Unfortunately we will never know what its ultimate height was. The pyramid was demolished as a "pagan monument" when the Spaniards conquered Mexico early in the sixteenth century. But archeologists, boring a network of tunnels into the ruins, have been able to estimate the pyramid's enormous bulk and trace its periodic enlargements. To their surprise they found the first, innermost, pyramid's walls well preserved and beautifully decorated with frescoes.

Why would a people build one pyramid over another? There is a theory that building a new structure over an old one was tied into a time cycle.

Primitive people were obsessed with the need to divide time into periods. And many of the Indian tribes had systems for reckoning time. Some of these methods were fairly simple. On the other hand, the Mayan Indians developed a remarkable 365-day calendar consisting of eighteen months of twenty days each, plus five "unlucky" (Uayeb) days. But whether the Indian's calendar was simple or sophisticated, it served the all-important purpose of telling the people when religious rituals should take place.

Thus time marked off had a mystical significance for the Indians. At the end of certain time spans it was believed that a kind of renewal of the earth took place. And it was important that the Indians renew their own environment at the same time. Building a new pyramid over an old one may have been part of this renewal.

In any event, the practice resulted in the excellent preservation of some ancient architecture that might otherwise have been lost.

Working in Uaxactun, an ancient Mayan city, archeologists were exploring a rather drab and crumbled pyramid when they found a perfect jewel of a pyramid inside. The smaller pyramid was ornately covered with creamy white stucco, and when exposed to the tropical sun it seemed to burst into light. Flanking its staircase were eighteen handsome stucco-sculpture masks of the jaguar god, each eight feet high. It dated from the ear-

161

liest Mayan civilization, around 400 B.C., and was one of the oldest Indian pyramids ever found.

No one can guess how many undiscovered Indian pyramids may still be uncovered—not only hidden within larger pyramids, but buried in the jungle.

In Egypt the desert's shifting sands buried pyramids. In Mexico and Central America pyramids were quickly engulfed and hidden by the unchecked growth of lush jungle vegetation. And since the Indian pyramids did not stand alone, the great complex of buildings they were part of—entire cities and religious centers—were buried in the jungle with them.

One of the most extraordinary pyramids in Mexico was brought to light when the ancient city of El Tajin was reclaimed from the jungle. The city, covering an area of a thousand acres, was found buried beneath thick vegetation in the state of Vera Cruz. When work on its restoration began, in the 1930s, among the great complex of buildings found was the Pyramid of the Niches.

The pyramid was built in six tiers, the top of each tier overhung with decorative cornices. Hundreds of square niches were carved into the sides of the pyramid. The play of the sun against the pyramid causes a strange and dramatic checkerboard pattern of light and shadow. It is as awesome and compelling today as it must have been to the Indian who lived and worshipped in the ancient city.

*Carved panel from the Pyramid of
the Niches at El Tajin, Mexico.*

Pyramid of the Niches, El Tajin.

Many of these lost cities were large population areas, supporting a vast number of people in ancient times. Some, located near major trading routes, were important marketplaces. All were great religious centers.

Much of the populace, farmers, laborers, and craftsmen, may have dwelt outside the city. But the city itself was their true center. In it lived the nobles who ruled their secular life, the warrior chiefs who led them in battle, and most important of all, the hierarchy of priests who commanded their religious lives and conducted the elaborate rituals that dominated their existence.

To build these cities took an enormous amount of planning, skill, and hard labor. The Indians who built them had no wheel, no beasts of burden. Their only cutting tools were sharpened stone. The cities were great complexes of palaces, towers, plazas, marketplaces, temples, and pyramids. The buildings were handsomely decorated with frescoes, stone carvings, and sculpture.

Why did the Maya abandon them when the cities were still in their prime? This remains one of the great mysteries of Indian civilization. Modern archeologists do not know the answer. As they slowly reclaim the cities from the jungle, they find no traces of the people. All that remains are the magnificent structures the Maya built and then left for the jungle to take over.

Most of the buried cities discovered so far were

built by the Maya Indians. The oldest and one of the largest is Palenque. It was a great center of Mayan civilization for more than a thousand years until its people deserted it around A.D. 900

In 1773, an Indian making his way through heavy jungle in the Chiapas mountains saw traces of ruins beneath the vegetation. Later he reported his discovery to a priest.

Careful excavation of the city was begun in modern times. And in 1931 a Mexican archeologist, Alberto Ruz Lhullier, working on the restoration of a temple on top of one of the larger pyramids, made a startling discovery.

In the floor of one of the temple rooms was a large stone slab with finger holes in it. Raising it, he was amazed to see a steep, narrow stairway that led down into the pyramid. It was filled with rubble, obviously placed there to block intruders.

While this feature was common enough in Egypt, it was unheard of in Indian pyramids.

Clearing the staircase, the excavators found that it went down partway to a landing, then changed direction, and descended to a total depth of about sixty feet, where it ended in a passage blocked with a stone wall.

When the wall was removed, they found the skeletons of six young men in front of a large stone door. Undoubtedly they were guardians sacrificed to protect the entrance. Removing the stone door, the excavators looked down a short flight of steps into a vaulted chamber containing an enormous, elegantly carved sarcophagus. The walls of the room were decorated with stucco relief figures of the nine gods of the nine underworlds, each bearing the scepter of the Rain God and the shield of the Sun God. The drama of the chamber was heightened by a dazzling array of stalactites hanging from the ceiling, formed by water dripping for more than a thousand years through the limestone rock of the pyramid above.

When the magnificently carved and decorated stone cover was raised from the sarcophagus, they found the skeleton of a very tall man. He was wrapped in a crimson burial robe in which were placed many carved ornaments. He had been buried with a diadem of jade, a breastplate of jade beads, rings on every finger, a large piece of jade in each hand and one in his mouth, earrings, carved necklaces. Over his face was a jade mosaic mask with eyes fashioned from shell.

The man was probably a Mayan lord who once ruled Palenque. No one knows why his tomb was placed in a pyramid in a land where pyramids were not ordinarily used for tombs.

It is possible, of course, that other tombs may be found in Indian pyramids. But it seems unlikely, since a large number of pyramids have been explored and no other tombs found.

It appears quite clear that the Indians built their pyramids with their summit temples solely as settings for the elaborate religious rituals to the gods who dominated their lives.

Much of this ritual revolved around sacrifice and the use of human blood. In Indian worship blood was a vital force. It had a special magic, and a constant supply was demanded by the gods.

To some extent, gods could be appeased by blood individuals drew from their own bodies. Cuts were made in the lower lip, tongues, and the cheeks, or earlobes were frayed, and the blood collected and smeared on the idol of the god whose help was needed. Blood from the penis had special magic and often the foreskin was frayed, or cuts were even made in the center of the penis to provide this special blood favored by the gods.

Still, blood obtained by self-imposed wounds was a mere trickle of what the gods demanded. The Sun God, for example, could be kept alive only by human blood, since the blood of man came from the sun and the life of the sun was the hearts of men. And the War God, Huitzilopochtoli, who led the way into battle in the form of a hummingbird, had to be maintained by a constant supply of blood.

This required human sacrifice. Victims met their sacrificial deaths in a number of ways, none pleasant. Probably the least painful was one Mayan rite. The victims—children as well as men and women—were thrown into a cenote, or sacred well.

However, this did not appease the Sun God, who

needed flowing blood, nor the bloodthirsty God of War. So the most common sacrificial death was also the bloodiest, and the pyramid with its steep stairway leading up to the temple made a dramatic setting for the spectacle.

The ritual, accompanied by the beating of drums, started at the base of the pyramid, with priests and those "chosen" for sacrifice slowly climbing the stairs to the top. There, in front of the temple, the victim was seized by four priests. Each held a limb, and the victim's back was arched over a sacrificial stone so that his chest was high and exposed. A fifth priest split open his chest with a sharpened stone, tore out his heart, and placed it still beating in a sacrificial bowl and offered it to the god. The drama was capped by rolling the victim's bleeding body down the flight of stairs to the base of the pyramid where, needless to say, a large audience watched.

Some of the victims ascended the stairs willingly to be sacrificed. They believed that the moment their hearts were torn out, they joined the god in his world beyond. Some were chosen for sacrifice a year in advance and treated with special favors and honor while waiting for the ritual.

But it was impossible to find enough willing victims among the populace to satisfy the insatiable blood thirst of the gods. So thousands each year were forced to climb the stairs to be sacrificed.

This was often the fate of prisoners taken in battle.

It was said that when the number of victims from other sources ran low, an Indian nation sometimes attacked a weaker neighbor, just to take prisoners for sacrificing to the gods. These wars waged for the sole purpose of obtaining sacrificial victims were known as "Flower Wars."

All this was to come to an end after the Spanish Conquest.

Cortes landed in Yucatan in 1519, supplied with soldiers and horses, firearms and gunpowder. The sixteenth century was an era of great territorial expansion for the empires of Europe. And Cortes came to the New World on a mission of conquest and colonization in the name of his King, Charles V of Spain.

Cortes's immediate goal was the acquisition of treasure, especially gold and silver to fill the coffers of the king. But beyond that, his mission was to wipe out the pagan religion of the Indians and establish Christianity in its place.

The Indians parted with their gold and silver. These they could live without. But they could not live without their religion.

Their gods directed their lives. Their gods gave them the sun, the rain, the land, everything needed to sustain life. The gods told them when to plant, when to reap, when to make war, when to make peace. Ritual worship of their gods was part of almost every act of daily living. Without their religion there would be no life.

Cortes saw that to establish Christianity, he had to conquer the people.

The Indians fought with bows and arrows and poles tipped with sharpened stones. Even so, the Spaniards with their horses and firearms did not find the Indians easy to subdue as they marched through Mexico to capture the Aztec capital, Tenochtitlan. The Aztecs were fierce and crafty warriors.

Once, when the Spaniards suffered a setback in their attack on the capital, they camped just outside the city to rest and regroup. Some of their men had been killed, many wounded, sixty-two had been captured by the Indians.

It was late afternoon as they watched the city for some sign of action. Tenochtitlan's beautiful towers and temples, and its great pyramid, which dominated the city, were all bathed in golden sunlight.

The quiet was broken by the throb of drums coming from the pyramid's temple. The soldiers saw a long procession led by the priests ascending the staircase. Ten of the men in the procession were white-skinned—their captive comrades. With helpless horror the Spaniards watched while each captive was stretched on the sacrificial stone, his chest split open, his heart torn out, and the victim hurled down the steep staircase. For the soldiers the night that followed was one of anguish and grieving. It came to be known, ever after, as "The Night of Sorrows."

Later, on the pyramid's same stairs, the Spaniards waged a fierce battle with the Aztecs all the way to the pyramid's summit. The Spaniards triumphed and every Aztec not slain was pitched to his death over the side of the pyramid. The victors then set fire to the temple.

In the weeks that followed, the entire city suffered the same fate of death and destruction. It was one of the longest and bloodiest sieges ever fought in the New World. The proud, warlike Aztecs and their young emperor repeatedly refused Cortes's appeals to surrender. Cortes knew that only by destroying them could he conquer them.

Most of the population perished. The once magnificent Aztec city, which Cortes pronounced the most beautiful city in the world when he first saw it, was reduced to great smoldering ruins. Cortes raised the Christian cross and the banner of Seville on the ruins. And in time a new city, without pyramids and other pagan monuments, was built on its site. Today it is the modern metropolis Mexico City.

After the Aztec nation was conquered, Cortes moved south to conquer the Maya. Their empire spread from Yucatan down through what are now Guatemala and northern Honduras.

The conquest of the Maya was a different story.

The Maya were a highly civilized people with a culture that had begun to flower in the fourth or fifth century B.C. They were literate, with a well-developed language and hieroglyphic writing. They were magnificent builders, fine artists and craftsmen.

But for several hundred years before the Con-

171

quest, their civilization had been steadily on the wane. By the time the Spaniards arrived, the Mayan empire was weak and divided. The people lived in widely scattered areas. The Maya could not offer the strong, united opposition that Cortes had encountered from the powerful, integrated Aztecs of Mexico. Each Mayan city stood alone in its defense against the invaders. The Mayan Indians fought bravely and desperately. But eventually every city fell and the Spaniards took over.

They killed the nobles and chieftains who would not collaborate, and took a large part of the male population into slavery. The priests were deposed, their manuscripts burned.

When the Conquest was over, the ancient Mayan way of life was ended.

But their culture would survive long after the Spaniards were gone. Today the Mayan people still speak their ancient tongue. And the culture of their ancestors lives on in the objects of beauty they create from materials at hand—clay and stone, fiber and wood.

For all the Indian pyramid builders, Mexican and Mayan, much was destroyed. But much that they built remains to tell us of their ancient civilizations.

Nothing still standing speaks more eloquently of their past than the pyramids.

12
Pyramids and Mystics

Many hundreds of years after the Egyptians who built them and those who robbed them were gone, the pyramids became shrouded in mysticism and superstitions. Fanciful theories were invented to explain how the pyramids had been built. Men could not believe that so complicated a structure, so enormous in size, could have been built without supernatural help.

One theory was that they were a result of sorcery. As early as the twelfth century a famous traveler, Rabbi Benjamin ben Johnah of Navarre, wrote from Egypt, "The pyramids which are seen here are constructed with witchcraft."

Another theory, supported by several reputable Egyptologists as late as the mid-nineteenth century, was that the knowledge necessary for their building was given by divine revelation. The same God who told Noah how to build the Ark had shown the ancient Egyptians how to build the pyramids.

Some advocates of the divine-revelation theory believed the pyramids were not built by the Egyptians at all. They were built by men from Christian lands. The God of the Bible, the only true deity, they said, would not have imparted divine knowledge to the idolatrous Egyptians, who worshiped false gods.

There were even theories that mighty and marvelous beings from other planets had landed mysteriously on earth to build the pyramids, only to vanish without any trace.

During the Middle Ages various superstitions were attached to the pyramids. People believed they were haunted by dangerous ghosts and evil spirits. According to an Arabian legend, the Great Pyramid was the dwelling place of wicked sirens whose mystic powers lured people inside, then drove them mad.

There were cults, especially popular in the seventeenth and eighteenth centuries, whose members believed that within the Great Pyramid divine or supernatural communication was possible. They told of receiving spiritual messages that revealed secrets of the past and foretold the future. Apparitions conveyed omens and prophecies. Mysterious voices spoke to them, imparting supernatural wisdom.

While the visits of ghosts and other apparitions

174

Tourists of today at Giza.

have long since been discounted, strange experiences in pyramids have been reported from reliable sources.

In 1839 the English scientist J. S. Perring was working in a passageway buried deep inside the Bent Pyramid. Suddenly a strong, fresh wind began to blow. Perring and his workmen were astounded. They were in an enclosed area, far from any air currents. As the wind continued, they searched for its source, without success. The wind continued to blow for two days. At times it blew so hard it was difficult to work. Then the wind stopped as mysteriously as it had started. Perring was never able to find its source or explain the phenomenon.

A modern archeologist, Ahmed Fakry, reported in the 1950s that unexplained sounds can frequently be heard in this same passageway.

Napoleon Bonaparte sensed something mysterious about the Great Pyramid, centering around the King's Chamber. Bonaparte requested his aides to leave him alone in the King's Chamber when he visited the pyramid in 1799. He was greatly agitated, pale and shaken, when he came out. One aide asked him if he had experienced anything strange. Napoleon replied that he did not want to comment on it, nor did he want the incident ever mentioned again.

Many years later on St. Helena, toward the end of his life, Napoleon brought up the subject himself. Then he looked at his companion, shook his head, and said, "No, no. There is no use speaking of it. No one would ever believe me."

Today a number of people probably would believe him—people who are convinced that something related to the pyramid shape causes unusual things to happen inside a pyramid.

Interest in the subject was sparked when another Frenchman, M. Bovis, visited the King's Chamber 150 years after Bonaparte. Bovis noticed in a garbage can carcasses of dogs and cats that had wandered into the pyramid and died there.

The bodies, he said, had never decayed—they

were dried out but lifelike. Bovis wondered if the pyramid form could be responsible for this unusual desiccation.

He built a small pyramid of wood with a base nine feet square in the exact ratio to the Great Pyramid, and oriented it on the same true-north axis. On a platform directly under the pyramid's apex, approximately where the King's Chamber would be, he placed a freshly dead cat. In a matter of days, the cat's body was completely dried out. Bovis then turned to other things that ordinarily spoil very quickly, such as the brains of cattle. These too, he insisted, dried out without any deterioration.

These experiments were not done in a monitored and controlled laboratory situation. But when Bovis reported his results, people in Europe and the United States became excited and started pyramid experiments of their own.

One of the first and better publicized of these was a radio engineer in Czechoslovakia, K. Drbal, who experimented with stainless steel razor blades. Such a blade has a crystal structure that breaks down with use. Drbal claimed that a used blade, placed in a pyramid, would return to its original structure and be sharp again. He said he could shave with one blade as many as two hundred times if he placed it back in the pyramid after each shave.

Many people believed Drbal and he turned his claims into a commercial success by manufacturing and selling cardboard pyramids for home use. And though Cheops's pyramid, which served as his model, was more than four thousand years old, Drbal was granted a Czechoslovakian patent (number 91304) for his "Cheops's Pyramid Razor Blade Sharpener."

In the United States early experiments were mostly with organic materials. The claims made were as beguiling as Drbal's claims for razor blades. Milk was said to stay fresh for almost a week, when it separated into curds and whey without spoiling. Sometimes the milk in the pyramid turned into yogurt. Samples of the same milk placed in the same room but outside the pyramid, however, were said to mold in a few days.

The assumption was that milk and other foods did not spoil because bacteria did not develop—or at least development was sharply curtailed—in a pyramid. Solid foods did dehydrate, however. A bunch of grapes dried up into raisins. A piece of raw meat became dried beef in about six weeks. Ham baloney dried without spoilage and was allegedly edible.

Foods kept in pyramids for a short time were said to improve in flavor. They tasted fresher than when they were placed there. Spices and herbs became more pungent. Tough cuts of meat marinated in a pyramid for just a few hours became succulent and tender. But all this pyramid magic worked only on natural foods. Foods that depended on artificial flavorings for tastiness became flat and unacceptable.

Water, it was claimed, benefited by pyramid storage, becoming sweeter, purer. Foods cooked in it had more flavor. Plants watered with it flourished. And bathing in it made the skin glow and improved one's complexion.

It was reported that the germination of seeds could be speeded up by 50 percent if sown in a pyramid. Even outside a pyramid, if seeds were planted in flats with pyramid-shaped covers of glass, they purportedly grew faster than seeds from the same package grown under glass covers of other shapes.

The validity of all these claims was questioned. Among other things it was pointed out that the tests were unreliable. They were not conducted under scientific or controlled conditions. There were no known facts or reasons for endowing the pyramidal form with special powers.

But the cultists who believe in its power say the shape of the pyramid creates a mysterious force—a field of energy—and therein lies its magic.

Models vary in size, and the builders say various materials may be used—cardboard, wood, glass, nonporous plastic, but not metal. It is said that metal doesn't work because its components are inimical to the energy field of the pyramid form.

But to function effectively, regardless of material or size, the pyramid must be built in the same form as the Great Pyramid of Giza, with the same true-north axis alignment. Some purists contend that the model must be in exact proportion to the Great Pyramid down to the smallest fraction of an inch. However, most builders agree that small deviations are harmless and permissible. This compromise is lucky for all the amateur pyramid builders who are neither higher mathematicians nor master craftsmen.

Believing that the pyramid's mysterious form could enhance the quality of inanimate objects, the pyramid builders asked: Why wouldn't it be beneficial for the animate, especially human beings? This posed a problem of construction. While it was fairly simple to build a small pyramid for a bowl of milk or a potted plant, a pyramid for people would have to be big enough to accommodate at least a chair or a cot. It would require space in a room in the house or on the property out of doors. However, a number of people have built or bought pyramids for their own use and seem to be very happy with them.

In a pyramid they say they sleep more peacefully, wake up more rested. Even a short nap in a pyramid restores them. People who are nervous or tense claim that in the pyramid they become calm. An overactive child, parents report, is more tractable after spending some time in a pyramid.

Students claim they can study more effectively in a pyramid. Meditation is said to be deeper and more meaningful. And people trying to work out knotty problems say they can think more clearly and productively in a pyramid.

The idea that one's thought processes are improved in a pyramid is not a twentieth-century notion. A group of stargazers in the Middle Ages held their meetings in the Great Pyramid because they believed it was a source of wisdom that mysteriously expanded their intellectual powers.

Some people attribute physical healing powers to their pyramids, asserting that chronic headaches, sinus congestion, arthritis, and other ailments have improved or disappeared after regular periods spent in one. Incidents of extraordinarily rapid healing of broken bones have been reported.

Skeptics point out that people who go into a pyramid expecting to feel better, think better, sleep better, will probably do so. Ailments cured, they say, might have been psychosomatic, or would have disappeared or gone into remission without pyramid sitting. And as for broken bones, any orthopedic doctor has records of patients whose fractures healed remarkably fast for some natural reason.

The skeptics also say that if a person went to the trouble and expense of buying or building a pyramid large enough for a person to use, he wouldn't want to admit that it was a failure, that he had had no "feedback." The twentieth-century pyramid builders simply believe what they want to believe.

There is no evidence that the ancient Egyptians who built the pyramids ever invested the shape with any power or magic. The pyramid was a dramatic and imposing form they created for the tombs of their pharaohs. However, archeologists, seeking to explain how the pyramidal form came into being, believe it may have had mythical or religious origins.

One is based on an early Egyptian belief that the world began when a mound of earth, rising to a peak, emerged from the waters of chaos. On this island the universe and all life was created.

A second, more literal theory is that the ancient Egyptians saw the shape in a stone used by other Near Eastern people in their own religious rites. Unique and roughly pyramidal in form, it was known as a *betyl stone*. Because of its remarkable shape and its rarity, it was thought to have supernatural significance. While it was not found in Egypt, the Egyptians, sailing to other shores for purposes of trade, undoubtedly had seen the betyl stone.

Another, and in many ways the most tempting, explanation is that the pyramid shape was inspired by the sun itself. Today, on rare occasions when there is a stormy cloud cover above the Egyptian desert, spectators marvel at the sight of the sun's rays breaking through, forming a triangular pattern of light from sky to earth.

This spectacle must surely have been witnessed by the ancient Egyptians. And what more fitting tomb for their pharaoh could they devise than a stone replica of the sun's radiant pattern? From its broad base on earth, the tomb would rise high in pointed glory, dominating the earth below. It would be the first object lighted by

Fig. 14. The idea of the pyramidal form may have come to the ancient Egyptians from a rare spectacle in the western sky above the desert. Late on a cloudy winter afternoon the sun's rays pierce the clouds, striking down in great triangles of light that approximate the angle of a true pyramid.

183

the Sun God in the morning, and the last to receive the god's golden rays at the end of the day.

Whether the idea of the pyramid's form came from a mythical island, a stone, the rays of the sun, or the mind of a genius, the ancient Egyptians who invented it gave the world a mighty symbol. For many centuries the pyramid has been used as a symbol by secret societies throughout the world. It appears on the reverse side of the Great Seal of the United States. Many Americans see it and touch it every day—it is pictured on the one-dollar bill.

Today, almost five thousand years after the first pyramid was built, the shape continues to symbolize strength, power, permanence. And the pyramids, rising in splendid symmetry from the desert to the sky, are surely the most magnificent monuments ever built by man.

Bibliography

Reisner, George Andrew. *Mycerinus, The Temples of the Third Pyramid at Giza.* Cambridge, Mass.: Harvard University Press, 1931.

Reymond, Eve A.E. *The Mythical Origin of the Egyptian Temple.* New York: Barnes & Noble, 1969.

Smyth, Charles Piazzi. *Our Inheritance in the Great Pyramid.* London: A. Strahan & Company, 1864.

Strabo. *The Geography of Strabo, VIII.* Translated by H.L. Jones. Cambridge, Mass.: Loeb Classical Library, Harvard University Press.

Vyse, Howard and J.S. Perring. *Operations Carried on at the Pyramids of Gizeh in 1837.* London: J. Fraser, 1840–42.

Winlock, Herbert Eustis. *The Rise and Fall of the Middle Kingdom in Thebes.* New York: Macmillan, 1947.

Bibliography for the American Pyramids of Mexico and Central America

Blacker, Irwin. *Cortes and the Aztec Conquest.* New York: American Heritage, 1965.

Díaz del Castillo, Bernal. *The Discovery and Conquest of Mexico.* New York: Farrar Straus & Cudahy, 1956.

Peterson, Frederick A. *Ancient Mexico.* New York: Putnam, 1959.

Prescott, William Hickling. *The History of the Conquest of Mexico.* Abridged and edited by C. Harvey Gardiner. Chicago: The University of Chicago Press, 1966.

Simon, Kate. *Mexico, Places and Pleasures.* Garden City, N.Y.: Doubleday, 1965.

Smith, Bradley. *Mexico—A History in Art.* New York: Harper & Row, 1968.

Stuart, George E. and Gene S. Stuart. *The Mysterious Maya.* Washington, D.C.: National Geographic Society, 1977.

Thompson, John Eric. *The Rise and Fall of Maya Civilization.* Norman: The University of Oklahoma Press, 1966.

Von Hagen, Victor Wolfgang. *The Ancient Sun Kingdoms of the Americas.* London: Thames & Hudson, 1962.

Von Hagen, Victor Wolfgang. *World of the Maya.* New York: New American Library, 1960.

Willey, Gordon. *An Introduction to American Archeology.* Englewood Cliffs, N.J.: Prentice-Hall, 1966.

Index

```
932    Pace, Mildred Mastin
P
       Pyramids
```

DATE		
OCT. 2 0 1987	APR. 2 0 1987	
OCT. 2 9 1987		
OCT. 2 6 1988		
OCT. 1 8 1989		
OCT. 1 9 1990		
OCT. 3 1 1991		
DEC. 5 1992		
OCT 1 0		

© THE BAKER & TAYLOR CO.